THE VICTORIA HISTORY OF HAMPSHIRE

CLIDDESDEN, HATCH AND FARLEIGH WALLOP

Alison Deveson and Sue Lane

First published 2018

A Victoria County History publication for the Institute of Historical Research

© The University of London, 2018

ISBN 978-1-912702-00-8

Typeset in Minion Pro by Jessica Davies Porter

CONTENTS

LIST OF ILLUSTRATIONS

All photographs are by the authors, John Deveson and Jennie Butler unless otherwise stated. All maps are drawn by Cath D'Alton and © University of London unless otherwise stated.

Figures

Maps

FOREWORD

FOR MORE THAN 500 YEARS my family has owned land in Farleigh Wallop, Cliddesden and Hatch. The principal residence at the heart of the estate today, Farleigh House, was the family seat from 1486 through to 1661, from 1937 to 1950 and then again from 1989 to 2014. A programme of restoration and improvement of the building was begun in 1987 and was completed in 1990. The gardens and grounds too have been restored and transformed. The house has just entered a new incarnation as a fully staffed 'house for hire'. The parish church, St Andrew's Farleigh Wallop, continues in its long tradition of serving as a memorial chapel to the Wallop family.

My grandfather, the 9th earl, began the modernisation of the farms and the provision of housing for estate workers in the 1920s. I myself have lived at Farleigh since 1976. During this time I have seen this parish and the neighbouring parishes develop in different ways reflecting modern alternative land use, and I have witnessed considerable changes in agriculture, both practically and economically.

I am delighted that the authors have undertaken the task of researching and recording the history of an area with so many personal associations, interests and concerns, as well as the wider history of the local communities. They have worked extensively in the Wallop family archives (now in the care of Hampshire Record Office), in the National Archives and they have examined ecclesiastical and civil records from 1086 onwards. They have involved many local people in this project and have had the help of various experts in their fields. I commend this history not only to all who know and care for the area but also to those from further afield.

This volume forms part of the Victoria History of the Counties of England (VCH), which originated in the time of Queen Victoria. It follows similar histories of Mapledurwell, Steventon and Medieval Basingstoke. The current project aims to write parish histories covering a wider range of people and topics than in the earlier publications. In Hampshire, perhaps the greatest changes since the first VCH volumes appeared have been in Basingstoke and its environs. That is why the Hampshire team of historians and volunteers chose to start their research in this part of the county. These are works which combine high academic standards with an approachable and fascinating picture of history at a local level.

Earl of Portsmouth DL

ACKNOWLEDGEMENTS

THE PARISH HISTORIES OF CLIDDESDEN, Hatch and Farleigh Wallop add to the three already published as part of the new Victoria County History of Hampshire. Cliddesden and Farleigh Wallop were selected for publication as examples of parishes which still had resident manorial lordship and the records of the Wallop family, earls of Portsmouth from 1743, provide a particularly rich source of material. As with other rural parishes on the outskirts of Basingstoke the interaction between town and country has been significant, from the time of prosperity brought by the woollen industry in the 1500s, to the pressures in the countryside caused by the growth of the town since the 1960s.

This book owes a great deal to the VCH Hampshire team. Wills and inventories relating to Cliddesden and Farleigh Wallop were transcribed by the wills group which meets regularly in Basingstoke and some of whose members read and commented on the text. Joan Wilson researched and wrote the section on Cliddesden School, Mary Oliver and Roger Ottewill contributed paragraphs on early settlement in Cliddesden and the Congregational chapel at Farleigh Wallop respectively. Bill Fergie and Edward Roberts advised on buildings, Gavin Bowie commented on the agricultural sections and Jean Morrin, project leader, provided guidance throughout the writing of these parish histories. Sarah Lewin of Hampshire Record Office gave particular help with the chapters on religious history and, with colleagues, made available invaluable expertise and resources.

Lord and Lady Portsmouth, Lord Lymington and the Revd Stephen Mourant provided local information, as did Chris Allen, Robert Applin, Paul Beevers, David and Barbara Evans, Irene Holloway, Greta Iddeson, John Paterson and Ken and Pat Rampton. They were all generous with their time and knowledge, as were many other local residents. Permission to reproduce illustrations is gratefully acknowledged from the following bodies and individuals: Basingstoke and Deane Borough Council, Hampshire Record Office, the Museum of English Rural Life at the University of Reading, Wessex Archaeology, Winchester Cathedral Library, Lord and Lady Portsmouth, Portsmouth Estates, Margaret Casserley, Edward Roberts and Elizabeth Vickers. John Deveson and Jennie Butler contributed many photographs.

Financial contributions from individuals towards the costs of publication have been much appreciated, as was a grant made by the VCH Counties Fund towards the production of maps. The team at VCH central office at the Institute of Historical Research, University of London, has offered welcome guidance, particularly Adam Chapman (Editor) and Matthew Bristow (Research Manager). Jessica Davies Porter (Publications Manager) managed the production of the publication. We extend our thanks to them all.

CLIDDESDEN AND FARLEIGH WALLOP ARE small adjacent parishes lying on the slopes of the chalk downlands to the south of Basingstoke and separated from it by the M3 motorway from London to Southampton, which forms their north-western boundaries. Cliddesden, the larger settlement, is two miles from the centre of Basingstoke, its mix of old farm buildings and houses of all periods from the 16th to the 21st centuries reflecting its historic development. The village's continuing expansion is due in no small part to the proximity of the town with its excellent transport links. A steep hill leads south-westwards from Cliddesden to Farleigh Wallop where the small hamlet tucked away along a tree-lined avenue is clustered around Farleigh House, the seat of the earls of Portsmouth. Farleigh Wallop retains its rural character.

Hatch, a separate parish until the late 14th century, was a detached part of Cliddesden parish for well over five centuries before being joined with Farleigh Wallop. Hatch Warren Farm, which lay west of Cliddesden village and immediately to the north of the M3 motorway, was absorbed within Basingstoke and developed for suburban housing in the late 20th century. Its history appears in both sections of this book and its most recent development will be included in a forthcoming volume on Basingstoke.

The history and activities of the parishes are closely intertwined. They have a common manorial descent from the 15th century onwards, and were consequently managed as components of a single estate under the lordship of the Wallop family (earls of Portsmouth since 1743), although most of the lords have been non-resident until the 20th century. In 2017, Farleigh Wallop was wholly owned by Portsmouth Estates and Cliddesden largely so. In 2017 the land in both surviving parishes was run as a single unit from an estate office at Farleigh House. The estates comprise farms in both parishes, with interlocking acreages and fields, and the geology, archaeology and land use of both parishes are broadly similar, both being mainly on chalk downland, although Farleigh Wallop mostly lies at a higher altitude than Cliddesden, and is more wooded. There are no apparent surface water courses in either parish but both have a number of man-made ponds. There were ancient churches in Cliddesden, Farleigh Wallop and Hatch, although Hatch church fell out of use in the second half of the 14th century. Cliddesden and Farleigh Wallop had their own rectors until 1579 when Farleigh Wallop was combined with Cliddesden in a benefice known as Cliddesden cum Farleigh, thus uniting the religious life of the two parishes for nearly four centuries until pastoral reorganisation in 1954. Nonconformity in the late 19th and the 20th century was represented by Methodist chapels in Cliddesden and a short-lived Congregational chapel in Farleigh Wallop. Cliddesden School is the school for Cliddesden, Farleigh Wallop and Ellisfield, but was built on land in Farleigh Wallop.

The parishes differ in several respects. Although they are so closely related, they were always in different hundreds. Cliddesden and Hatch in Basingstoke hundred, Farleigh

Wallop in Bermondspit hundred. Farleigh Wallop is an estate village, and there has been a manor house recorded from the 14th century, whereas Cliddesden had no manor house. Farleigh House, with its park, was visited by Elizabeth I in 1591 and rebuilt after a fire in the late 17th century. It is by far the most prominent building in the two parishes but settlement did not develop around it, and the limited number of modern houses are at a discreet distance from the house and its home farm. In the early 21st century, population, services and community activities were concentrated in Cliddesden, which has been more affected than Farleigh Wallop by its closer proximity to Basingstoke. Boundary changes resulting from transfers of Hatch in 1932, 1971 and 1985, allied with the expansion of Basingstoke, have produced greater fluctuations in the population of Farleigh Wallop than that of Cliddesden. In 2017 Farleigh Wallop – the smaller village – had a parish meeting whilst Cliddesden had a parish council.

CLIDDESDEN PARISH COVERS 455 HA. (1,124 a.) of rolling downlands, and is largely devoted to arable farming. The first evidence of human activity was at Swallick Farm in the south-east of the parish, but the village of Cliddesden developed along the north-western boundary and lies in a dry valley at an approximate height of 400 ft (122 m.) above sea level. The land rises on both sides of the village street, giving an enclosed feel to the settlement, and the large pond beside the staggered crossroads provides a central focal point. The buildings of Church Farm and Manor Farm are an integral part of the village though used mainly as housing and offices in the 21st century. The church of St Leonard, incorporating 12th century material, stands away from the centre of the village. Hatch, containing Hatch Warren Farm and lying to the west, was a detached part of Cliddesden parish until 1932.

Place-names and Farms

The manor of Cliddesden and its near neighbour and later detached portion, Hatch, were both in the hundred of Basingstoke. Both place-names have had variants, but their correct identifications are not in doubt. Variant spellings of Cliddesden have included Cleresden, Clereden, Cladisden, Cludsden, Cludesden, Cledesden, Cledisdon and Clidesdene.[1] Variants of Hatch have included Heche, Heccha and Hacche.[2] Hatch is Old English *hæcc*, 'gateway', but its association with a specific feature is not apparent. The 'dene' element in Cliddesden denotes a long narrow valley, but the origin of the first element is uncertain.[3]

The names of two farms in Cliddesden have varied. Manor Farm, positioned on rising ground south of the village centre, was occasionally called Upper Farm.[4] The demesne farm, originally called Cliddesden Farm, has also been known as Manor Farm, but was known since the early 20th century as Church Farm.[5] The modern names Manor Farm and Church Farm are used throughout this book, regardless of those in original documents, where maps, field names and acreages usually aid identification. The farm which succeeded the abandoned settlement at Hatch was named Hatch Warren Farm,[6] but the area as a whole was not called Hatch Warren until it was adopted as a ward name

1   *Domesday*, 115; *Pipe R 1166–7* (PRS 11), 190; Dugdale, *Mon.* VII, 1014; TNA, CP 25/1/205/15; CP 25/1/203/4; CP 25/1/204/9; *Rot. Hund.* II, 221.
2   *Domesday*, 120; *Pipe R 1166–7* (PRS 11), 189; TNA, CP 25/1/205/16.
3   Coates, *Place-names*, 88, 57.
4   HRO, 15M84/3/1/2/5.
5   HRO, 15M84/3/1/1/51; OS 1st edn 1:10,560, Hampshire sheet XVIII, 1877; OS 1912 edn, 1:10,560, Hampshire sheet XVIII SE, 1912.
6   Below, Cliddesden – Economic History.

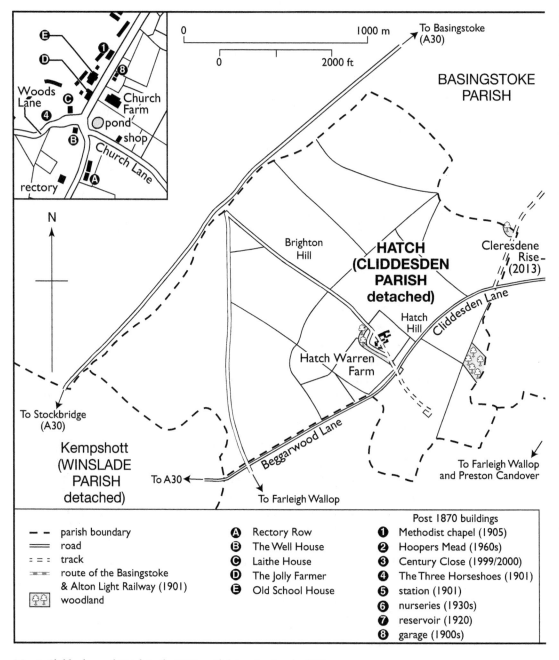

Map 1 *Cliddesden and Hatch in the 1870s with later structural additions.*

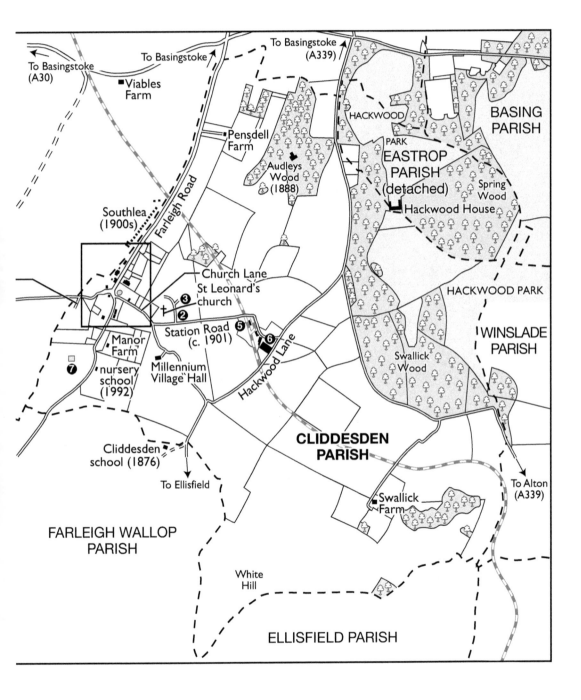

To Basingstoke (A30)

To Basingstoke

To Basingstoke (A339)

Viables Farm

HACKWOOD

BASING PARISH

Pensdell Farm

EASTROP PARISH (detached)

PARK

Spring Wood

Audleys Wood (1888)

Hackwood House

Southlea (1900s)

Farleigh Road

HACKWOOD PARK

Church Lane
St Leonard's church

WINSLADE PARISH

Station Road (c. 1901)

Hackwood Lane

Swallick Wood

Manor Farm

nursery school (1992)

Millennium Village Hall

CLIDDESDEN PARISH

Cliddesden school (1876)

To Ellisfield

Swallick Farm

To Alton (A339)

FARLEIGH WALLOP PARISH

White Hill

ELLISFIELD PARISH

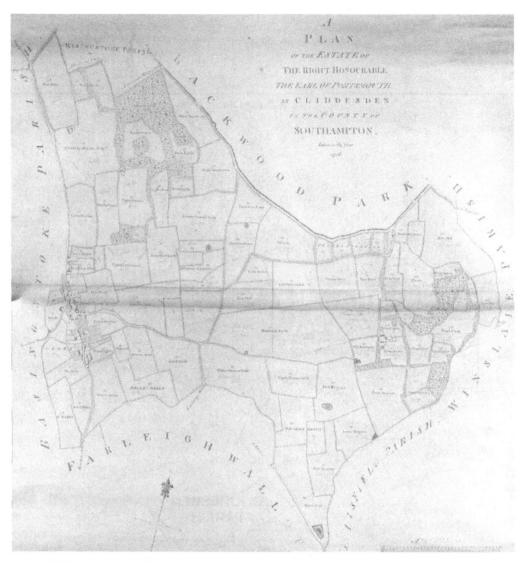

Map 2 *Cliddesden estate map, 1786.*

by Basingstoke and Deane Borough Council. This book uses the name Hatch except for specific references to the farm.

Boundaries and Area

Cliddesden parish was divided into two parts, divided by the wedge-shaped southern tip of Basingstoke parish's open fields. The eastern part contained the settlement of Cliddesden, the western part centred on Hatch, which was a separate manor until 1311 and formed a separate parish until the late 14th century, but was thereafter part of Cliddesden.[7]

The main part of Cliddesden had a much more irregular shape, defined to the north west by the Alresford and Preston Candover to Basingstoke road designated B3046 in 2018, which climbs a shallow, dry valley up the lower slopes of Farleigh Hill. The boundary then ascends, first east and then due south parallel and to the east of the road south to Ellisfield reaching its highest point on downland at White Hill. Cliddesden's southern boundary runs slightly south of the ridge of the hill, before turning due north just to the west of Winslade hamlet. A map of the Cliddesden estate dated 1786 shows that its boundary was almost identical with that of the main, eastern part of the parish in 1842 except that the north-eastern boundary of the estate followed the road from Basingstoke to Alton (now the A339) whereas that of the parish ran through Hackwood Park (created in 1223) in fact through Hackwood House itself.[8] Hatch was a relatively compact block of land, with a slightly irregular boundary where it abutted Farleigh Wallop parish. This portion had, as its north-western boundary, the Basingstoke to Winchester road, in 2017 the A30. Its north-eastern boundary abutted Basingstoke's open fields before reaching the lane now called Hatch Warren Way parallel to the M3. From there the boundary continued up a dry valley, south-south-west towards the head of that valley on the slopes of Farleigh Hill. From its southernmost point the boundary headed north as far as Hatch Warren farm before heading west along the 500 ft contour to meet the Winchester road at the meeting point of Woodbury Road and Cliddesden Lane, in 2017 marked by a roundabout.

The area of the parish (Cliddesden and Hatch combined) was stated as 1,884 a. in 1842 but in the early 1870s it was surveyed at 1,919 a. although there were no intervening boundary changes.[9] The 19th-century boundary was retained as the civil parish boundary after local government reorganisation in 1894 and was kept until 1932, when almost the whole of Hatch (695 a.) was transferred to Farleigh Wallop. At the same time, 252 a. were transferred from Cliddesden to Winslade parish, and the Cliddesden boundary was altered to run slightly west of the road from Basingstoke to Alton instead of through Hackwood Park.[10] A further 31 a. were transferred to Basingstoke borough, and as a result of these changes, the area of Cliddesden parish was reduced to 940 a.[11] The M3 motorway, opened in 1971, cut across the northern tip of the parish, with Cliddesden marginally increasing its area in 1985 when its north-western boundary was moved to the centre of the motorway.[12] The parish area was stated as 446 ha. (1,102 a.) in 1991 and as 455 ha. (1,124 a.) in 2001 after a small alteration in the boundary between Cliddesden and Farleigh Wallop south of Cliddesden school.[13]

7   Below, Cliddesden – Landownership, Religious History.
8   *VCH Hants* IV, 122; HRO, 15M84/MP7; 21M65/F7/53/1–2.
9   OS 1st edn 1:10,560, Hampshire sheets XVIII, 1877, XXVI, 1875. The schedule in HRO, 21M65/F7/53/1 states the area as 1,824 a. but the summary more accurately as 1,884 a.
10   OS Provisional edn 1: 25,000, sheet SU64, 1958.
11   County of Southampton Review Order: Ministry of Health Order no. 76235; *Census*, 1931, 1951.
12   Basingstoke and Deane (Parishes) Order, 1985; OS Pathfinder 1:25,000, sheet 1224, rev. 1987–8.
13   *Census*, 1991–2001.

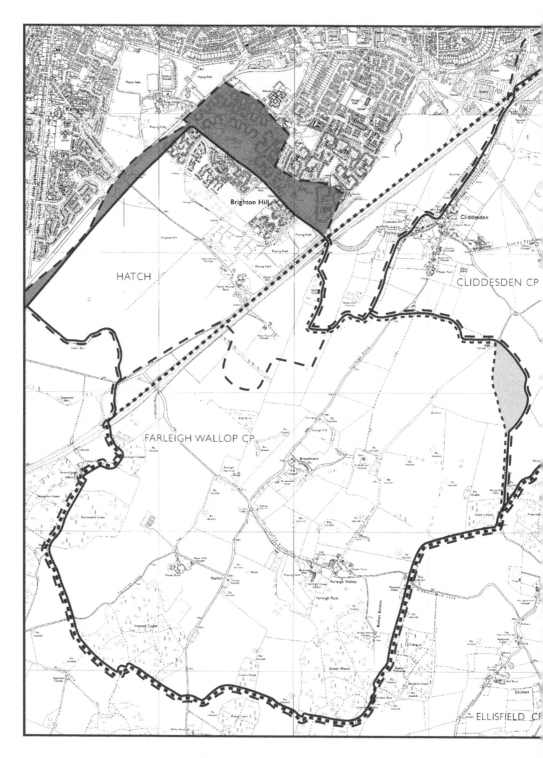

Map 3 *Cliddesden, Hatch and Farleigh Wallop showing boundary changes overlaid onto a 1:10,000 Ordnance Survey map.*

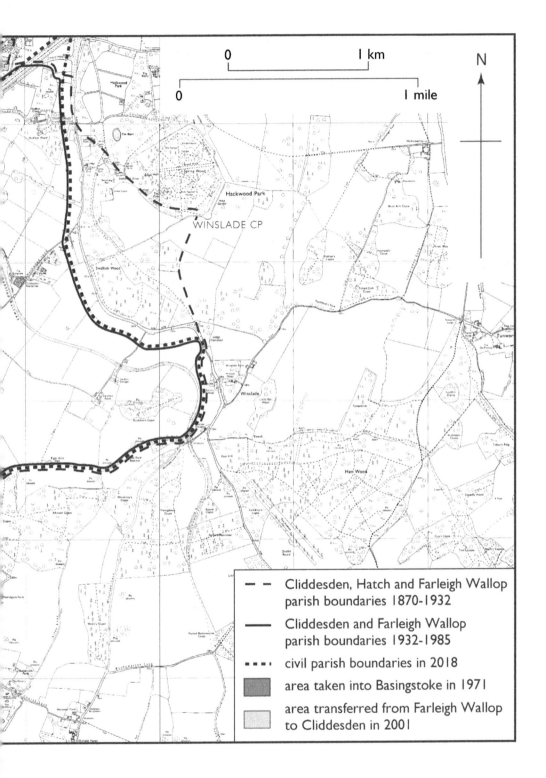

0					1 km			N

0							1 mile

WINSLADE CP

Hackwood Park

Winslade

Hen Wood

– – Cliddesden, Hatch and Farleigh Wallop
      parish boundaries 1870-1932

—— Cliddesden and Farleigh Wallop
      parish boundaries 1932-1985

▪ ▪ ▪ ▪ civil parish boundaries in 2018

█ area taken into Basingstoke in 1971

█ area transferred from Farleigh Wallop
    to Cliddesden in 2001

Landscape, Communications and Settlement

Landscape and Geology

The lower part of Cliddesden parish lies at about 400 ft (122 m.), with a gently
undulating landscape, in one fold of which is the village of Cliddesden. The landscape
rises more steeply up the valley which forms the boundary between Cliddesden and
Farleigh Wallop, and reaches a maximum height of 643 ft (196 m.) on the downland
of White Hill, where Farleigh Wallop and Cliddesden both meet the boundary with
Ellisfield to the south. The geology of this part of Cliddesden is upper chalk, except for
an area of clay with flints and loam overlying chalk along the upper slopes of White
Hill.[14] Hatch is also on upper chalk, reached by the more gradual slope of Hatch Hill,
and occupies a broad plateau above the south-western edge of Basingstoke, with a
maximum height of just under 600 ft (183 m.). A 240,000-gallon reservoir, which became
operational in 1907, is a feature of the landscape on the eastern slope of Hatch Hill. It
was constructed to supply water for Basingstoke and is filled by boreholes drilled into
the aquifer.[15] There is some woodland in the north of Cliddesden parish, in the vicinity
of the house known as Audleys Wood, and in the east at Swallick Farm, and there are
formal plantations in the part of Hackwood Park which lay in Cliddesden parish until
1932. In 2017 Cliddesden was predominantly under arable cultivation.

Communications

Roads, Carrier, Post

Two roads run through Cliddesden parish – the major road which links Basingstoke
with Alton (A339), and the minor road from Basingstoke via Preston Candover to
Alresford (B3406). The antiquity of these roads cannot be proved, but they were long-
distance routes by the 17th century and were included in tables of distances between
towns in road-books.[16] In the late 18th century they were 'notoriously impassable for any
other carriages but wagons, and for those only when drawn by a very powerful team of
horses'. In 1795 both roads were turnpiked under the same Act, with financial backing
from landowners who included the 2nd earl of Portsmouth though there is no evidence
for a toll gate in the parish.[17] They were disturnpiked in 1871.[18] Local traffic used the
lanes which traversed the parish, including Woods Lane, which crossed the southern
end of Basingstoke parish and linked the main part of Cliddesden with the detached

---

14   OS Geological maps of England and Wales 1:50,000 series, sheet 284, drift edn.
15   *The Times*, 22 Apr. 1907.
16   E.G. Box, 'Hampshire in early maps and early road-books', *Proc. Hants F.C.* 12 (1931), 226–32.
17   HRO, 44M69/G1/156–7.
18   HRO, 50M63/C7.

Figure 1 *Cliddesden landscape looking south towards White Hill. The line of trees on the horizon is the parish boundary with Ellisfield.*

part at Hatch.[19] Church Lane led east to the church, forking to ascend White Hill on the south and to descend via Hackwood Lane to Hackwood Park on the north. Tracks and footpaths provided direct access to the fields, the outlying farm of Swallick and the estate centre at Farleigh Wallop. No public carriers ever served Cliddesden, and the nearest post town during the 18th and 19th centuries was Basingstoke.[20]

Railway, Buses

A proposal in 1884 to build a railway between Basingstoke and Petersfield, routed through Cliddesden and Alton, came to nothing, but the Basingstoke and Alton Light Railway was completed in 1901. It passed through the parish on a similar route to that proposed in 1884 and was operated by the London and South Western Railway.[21] Although it was the first railway authorised under the Light Railways Act (1896) it was not the first to be completed. The railway line was intended as a relief measure to alleviate economic decline in rural north Hampshire, but it was not a financial success and was closed in 1917, in response to a Government appeal for railway material for use in France, and most of its track was lifted. By 1922, local landowners and farmers were campaigning for its reinstatement, and the line was reopened in 1924 but still failed to

---

19 The name is a corruption of Hoods, an adjacent field: HRO, 15M84/MP7.
20 *Parson and Parish*, 39–40; *PO Dir. Hants.*, 1855–67; *Kelly's Dir. Hants.*, 1859–89.
21 *London Gaz.*, 23 Nov. 1883, 5706–8; TNA, RAIL 1066/239–43; MT 6/1023/2.

Figure 2 *Cliddesden station shortly before closure.*

make a profit. Passenger services ended in 1932 but a goods service continued as far as Bentworth and Lasham until 1936.[22]

Cliddesden station was the first station south of Basingstoke, and was situated half a mile from the village centre, its site being a compromise between the wishes of the parish council and the technical requirements of the railway company. An access road, initially called New Road and then Station Road, linked the station with Hackwood Lane and Church Lane. The station building was a modest corrugated iron structure, but the station master was provided with a solid brick house, and there was a terrace of four cottages for railway staff.[23] The station was transformed into 'Buggleskelly' for the popular film *Oh Mr Porter!* in 1937 but the track removal had already begun and was complete by the end of the year.[24] The course of the line is still discernible in many places, and the cottages and the station master's house survive as private houses.

When the railway line was decommissioned in 1917, it was replaced by a temporary motor lorry service for goods from Herriard and Cliddesden to Basingstoke, and the increase in affordability and availability of motor transport during the 1920s was one of the reasons for the line's eventual failure. In 1927 the Venture Bus Company introduced a service from Basingstoke to the surrounding villages including Cliddesden, and a public bus service has continued ever since, operated by Stagecoach's Cango service in 2016.[25]

22   Dean and others, *Light Railway*, 9, 23, 52, 55–6, 74–6.
23   Ibid., 18–19, 87–90.
24   Ibid., 77–81.
25   Ibid., 53, 67–8; www3.hants.gov.uk/CANGO (accessed 5 Oct. 2016); Farleigh Wallop, Communications.

Settlement

Early Settlement

The earliest evidence of human activity in the parish occurs along the slopes of White Hill, and at Swallick Farm, close to the edge of the clay-with-flints deposits on the crest of the hill. The flint nodules in this deposit would have been an attractive source of raw material and explain the concentration of Palaeolithic and Mesolithic sites in this vicinity. Hand-axes, cores and flakes have been found at these sites.[26] An area south of Swallick Farm was also a flint-working site in the Mesolithic period, with tranchet axes, cores, a pick and microliths found during field-walking.[27] Flint-working continued into the Neolithic period, and very large quantities of flint have been recovered, making this location one of the most prolific in the district.[28] Another extensive Neolithic flint-working site spread over the slopes of Hatch Hill. Numerous implements – scrapers, fabricators, borers, axes and arrowheads – are recorded, and one stone axe-head from Devon or Cornwall.[29] There is almost no recorded activity from the Bronze Age apart from a ploughed-out barrow on the hillside on the eastern edge of the parish.[30]

Later prehistoric settlement was uncovered during housing development at Hatch, which was extensively studied in 1984–6 in advance of building. Aerial photographs, field-walking, geophysical survey and selective excavation yielded much information.[31] A series of enclosures was occupied from the early Iron Age until the Roman Conquest, with evidence of metalworking, weaving, stockrearing and imported and locally made pottery. There was no direct evidence for houses, but an iron latch-lifter and a key were discovered. There were two other groups of enclosures and a number of ditches, so this was a well-organised and utilised area of land.[32]

The archaeological record for the Iron Age and Roman periods in the current Cliddesden parish is very slight. There are the remains of a Celtic field system on the north-west slopes of White Hill, and a Roman brooch, bracelet and toothpick have been found in fields outside the village.[33] They are in the same general area as crop marks on aerial photographs, which suggests that there may have been an occupation site. Field-walking in 2006 over this area yielded many fragments of abraded pottery from the late Iron Age and Roman periods and also medieval to modern, resulting from the practice of manuring the fields.[34]

The documentary evidence for the medieval settlement of Hatch was reinforced by the excavation of one of the series of enclosures on the area developed for housing.[35] It

---

26 Hants HER 59201, 20301, 20294.
27 Hants HER 20302.
28 Hants HER 20300, 20275.
29 Hants HER 20288–9.
30 Hants HER 20244.
31 Fasham and Keevill, *Brighton Hill*, 33–60.
32 Hants HER 33840, 33842, 33846, 55942.
33 Hants HER 20286; www.finds.org.uk, nos HAMP-460AE3, 4669A5, FE7CC0 (accessed 17 Oct. 2015).
34 Hants HER 36376.
35 Below, Cliddesden – Landownership, Religious History; Fasham and Keevill, *Brighton Hill* 77–151.

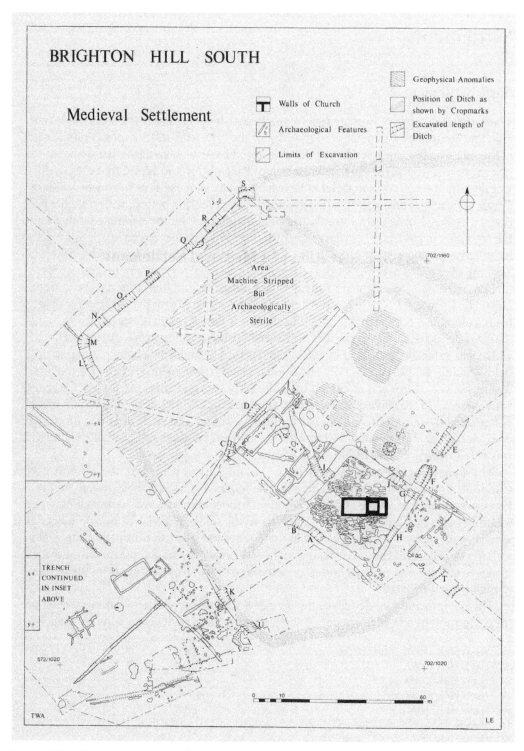

Figure 3 *Plan of the settlement at Hatch, showing all features and periods.*

was found to be the remains of a small group of houses round a two-cell, probably late Saxon, church within a fenced churchyard. There were 258 burials in the graveyard and nine within the church. Of these, 46 were excavated and dated between the 12th and 15th centuries suggesting that burials may have continued after the church was formally abandoned in the late 14th century.[36] A high proportion of the burials were of infants. Three phases of occupation in the settlement were recognised, the first of which was dated to the mid or late 11th century to the 12th century and consisted of two ranges of buildings north-west of the church and an area of open settlement to the south-west. The timber buildings were constructed with posts set in continuous slots. Around 1200, the ditches of the enclosures were dug, and the settlement was concentrated in the area south-west of the church. The construction technique was based on individual post holes with paired posts, a more sophisticated technique than previously, and at least four buildings were of a substantial size. The nature of the structures, the faunal remains, the high quality of the pottery assemblages and the association with a pre-Conquest church suggest that it was a manorial complex.[37] It was, however, a small settlement and the pottery evidence indicates that it was abandoned in the early 14th century. There was limited reoccupation at the end of the 14th century into the mid 15th century; the large number of sheep bones from one of the pits indicate that it was run as a sheep farm as documentary evidence shows that it was in the 16th century and later. The demolition of the church and the levelling of the site took place in the mid to late 15th century, and a well north of the church was filled in during this period. As the bottom of the well was not reached during excavation, it is not possible to say when it was first dug, but it may have served the community during the whole of its occupation.

Medieval and Later Settlement and Buildings

In 1086 the manor of Cliddesden had 16 tenant households, divided between villeins and bordars, and nine slaves. This suggests the existence of a number of small farms and smaller holdings in addition to land held in demesne.[38] Cliddesden also had a church, the peripheral position of which has led to speculation that it was once more central and that settlement has shifted to the cross roads that form its modern focus.[39] By 2017 no archaeological evidence had been found to support this. After the manor was united with Farleigh Wallop under the lordship of John Wallop (I) (d. 1486),[40] Farleigh House was the administrative centre for both manors, and the Cliddesden demesne farmhouse (Church Farm) and some of its lands were generally leased to a local farmer.[41] Its outbuildings, some of which have been converted to residential and commercial use, lie beside a large pond at the crossroads formed by the road from Basingstoke to Preston Candover (B3406) with Woods Lane on the west and Church Lane on the east. Cliddesden Down House, south of the crossroads, is the former rectory for the combined parishes of Cliddesden and Farleigh Wallop, and is probably a replacement for one or more previous

36 Below, Cliddesden, Religious History.
37 Hants HER 33612; Fasham and Keevill, *Brighton Hill*, 149–50.
38 *Domesday*, 115.
39 *Conservation Area* 11.
40 Below, Cliddesden – Landownership.
41 Below, Cliddesden – Economic History.

Figure 4 *Cliddesden pond in the early 1900s.*

rectories, which may not have been on the same site, but cannot have been far from the parish church.[42] These three buildings – demesne farmhouse, church and rectory – were the key elements of the settlement in the early modern period. The church, although not central, is not far from the crossroads.

Cliddesden village developed mainly in a linear form along the road from Basingstoke to Preston Candover, now called Farleigh Road but formerly Cliddesden Road or simply 'the village'.[43] The earliest surviving buildings are to be found associated with this early ribbon of development along the bottom of the valley, in particular close to the pond that marks the staggered crossroads in the middle of the village where Woods Lane and Church Lane meet the main street. The earliest surviving house appears to be a fine four-bay open-hall structure currently occupied as three cottages and numbered 1–3 Rectory Row. Its unusual S-shaped braces and herringbone infill brickwork suggest a mid 16th-century date and high status.[44] It is located immediately opposite the imposing 18th century Cliddesden Down House.[45] Four further thatched houses in this vicinity – Thatches, Yew Tree Cottage, The Well House and The Laithe House – exhibit varying amounts of timber framing and probably date from the 17th century, the period in which open halls in Hampshire were superseded by fully-floored houses at the rural vernacular level.[46] Although no longer thatched, and now rendered over later brickwork, Old School House is almost certainly an early 17th century lobby-entrance house.[47] To these early

42   Below, Cliddesden – Religious History.
43   *Census*, 1841–1901.
44   Hants HER 161.
45   Hants HER 2219.
46   Hants HER 2215–6; 2218, 2223; E. Roberts, *Hampshire Houses 1250–1700: Their Dating and Development* (Winchester, 2003), 214–7.
47   Hants HER 2214; below – Cliddesden, Social History.

Figures 5 and 6 *1–3 Rectory Row (above) and Yew Tree Cottage (below).*

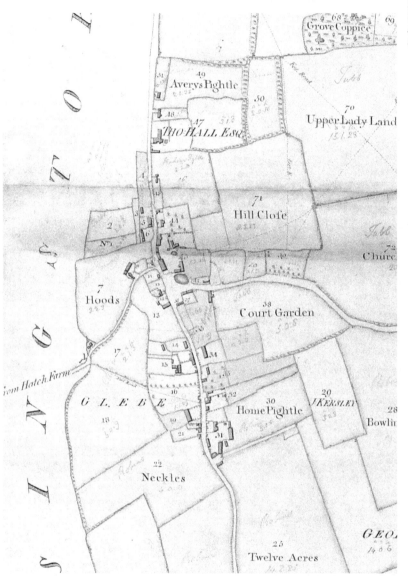

Map 4 *Cliddesden Street in 1786, showing the main area of settlement.*

houses can be added a further small group of thatched properties, 4–6 Rectory Row and a small cottage in Woods Lane, all perhaps of 18th-century date and the latter a rare example of cob construction.[48]

A small number of barns survive within the heart of the village, all timber-framed and probably all dating from the 17th or 18th centuries. The largest is the impressive roadside barn that was formerly part of the Church Farm complex but has been converted for business use and has a slate roof.[49] Opposite 1–3 Rectory Row another roadside barn is an outbuilding of Cliddesden Down House and has a corrugated steel roof instead of

48   Hants HER 2221, 2225.
49   Hants HER 50690.

Figure 7 *The Well House in 1980.*

its original thatch. Still thatched is the barn within the curtilage of The Laithe House in Woods Lane, now converted as a residential annexe.[50]

The two farms within the village are clearly on long-established sites, as evidenced by the early barn and listed staddle stone granary at Church Farm.[51] Replacement farmhouses on both sites are of 19th-century date, probably early in the century in the case of Manor Farmhouse and somewhat later in the century in the case of Church Farmhouse.[52] The long northern boundary to the garden of Church Farmhouse is defined by a cob wall, well protected from the elements by a clay tile capping.[53] Some agricultural buildings remain in use at Church Farm but, as with the Black Barn, former agricultural outbuildings have been retained or converted for business uses at Manor Farm. At Church Farm some residential infilling has also occurred.

The ready availability of new building materials during the 19th century gradually changed the character of the buildings in the village. Slates and tiles replaced thatch and a variety of industrially produced bricks replaced the generally softer local bricks, with the result that the previous uniformity of appearance gave way to a wider range of textures and colours. Notable but unlisted 19th-century houses in the centre of the village are Vine House and Farleigh Dene. At the northern end of the parish, the listed Audleys Wood was built in the 1880s in a vernacular revival style. Now greatly extended and used as a hotel, the original house is perhaps more notable for its interior fittings than for its

50   Hants HER 2224.
51   Hants HER 2217.
52   Hants HER 2222. Church Farmhouse is unlisted.
53   Hants HER 160.

Figure 8 *The Laithe House.*

external appearance. The interior is a treasure trove of salvaged timber work, including 17th-century chimneypieces, panelling of various types and an early 18th-century staircase. The front door is a fine 15th-century studded oak door, probably from a church. At the rear of the house is a large conservatory of *c.*1900 with a cast-iron frame.[54]

Development at the northern end of the village in the early years of the 20th century introduced a rather suburban feel. A 19th-century Methodist chapel was relocated from Basingstoke but was converted to residential use in the early 21st century. Its front elevation is of visually discordant ironstone in the Gothic style.[55] Adjoining it is a long line of semi-detached houses known as Southlea. They were built by the Basingstoke industrial firm of Wallis and Steevens to house their workers, and although not strictly within the parish boundary until 1985 have always been an integral part of the village.[56] Later in the 20th century, replacement and infill houses in the centre of the village have weakened the original vernacular homogeneity with a mixture of styles and materials.

A small field on the north side of Woods Lane was developed for houses shortly after the Second World War[57] and residential building has continued westwards on the south side of the lane in the 21st century, with a group of houses called Cleresdene Rise. On the eastern side of the village beyond the church, Hoopers Mead, constructed in the 1960s,

54   Hants HER 2220; Pevsner, *North Hampshire*, 227.
55   Below – Cliddesden, Religious History.
56   MERL, TR WAL, AD1/1; HRO, 58M74/BP128.
57   OS Provisional edn, 1:25,000, sheet SU64, 1958.

Figures 9 and 10 *Above, 10 Woods Lane and below, The Black Barn, a dominant feature in the village street.*

Figures 11 and 12 *Manor Farm House (above) and Church Farm House (below).*

and Century Close, built in the 1990s, provided retirement bungalows and low-cost housing. A small linear development on Hackwood Lane, intended for houses on large plots for servicemen returning from the First World War, has been largely redeveloped with houses dating between the 1950s and the 2000s.[58] The village hall, a replacement for one on the main street, was built in 1999 to commemorate the Millennium and stands isolated in Church Lane, on the eastern edge of the settlement. The primary school, opened in 1876, was built to serve a wider rural catchment area than Cliddesden and is located even further up the lane.[59]

Population

In 1086 the population of Cliddesden consisted of the households of at least six villeins, ten bordars and nine slaves.[60] Hatch had two villeins, no bordars and 11 slaves, making a combined total of 38 households indicating a population in the region of 160 in the two manors, plus those of the resident lords, if any.[61] Cliddesden's population was quite high and Hatch's around average, in comparison with other rural settlements in Hampshire.[62] The lordships of Cliddesden and Hatch were united in 1311 but they were enumerated separately in 14th-century taxation documents.[63] In 1327 there were ten inhabitants assessed for the lay subsidy in Cliddesden and six in Hatch.[64] The numbers were almost identical in 1333 (11 in Cliddesden, six in Hatch) although with some changes in the taxpaying population.[65] John de Valognes (II), lord of both manors, (d. 1337) was listed in both years. Cliddesden cannot have been immune from the effects of the 14th-century pestilences, although there is no direct evidence of any outbreak apart from the rapid succession of rectors between 1348 and 1350.[66] Hatch was a small, poor manor with a very low assessment in the lay subsidy of 1334[67] and 300 a. lay uncultivated in 1341.[68] Four jurors could still be found to attest to this, but Hatch suffered badly during the plague years and by 1378 was said to be completely depopulated. Some reoccupation of Hatch took place in the following centuries before it was absorbed by Basingstoke.[69]

Evidence for the population of Cliddesden from the 15th century to the early 19th century is sparse. The military skills and armour of 17 men were assessed in 1522, and 23 taxpayers were recorded in 1525.[70] There is a considerable overlap in the names in the two lists, but with more differences than might have been expected. Two of the 1525 taxpayers were female. Only ten taxpayers were assessed for the lay subsidies

58 *Design Statement*, 5–6.
59 Below, Cliddesden – Social History.
60 *Domesday*, 115.
61 Ibid., 120.
62 opendomesday.org (accessed 4 Mar. 2016).
63 Below, Cliddesden – Landownership.
64 *Hants Tax 1327*, 20.
65 TNA, E 179/242/15A, rot. 6.
66 Below, Cliddesden – Religious History.
67 Glasscock (ed.), *Subsidy 1334*, 118.
68 *Nonarum Inquisitiones*, 121.
69 Above, Cliddesden – Early Settlement; below, Cliddesden – Economic History, Religious History.
70 TNA, E 36/19, 168–9; E 179/173/183, rot. 5.

Figures 13 and 14 *Audleys Wood in the 1960s (above). Southlea, with Basingstoke in the background (below).*

of 1546 and 1547, falling to five in 1586.[71] The hearth tax return in 1665 recorded 21
taxpayers with chargeable hearths and five with unchargeable hearths, making a total
of 26 houses, fewer than in 1086.[72] Similar returns in 1673 and 1675 listed 23 and 26
households in those years respectively.[73] The numbers of communicants in the parish
were combined with those of Farleigh Wallop, and were estimated at 108 in 1603 and 110
in 1676.[74] By 1725 the estimated population of the two parishes was 170, which rose to
310 by 1788, for the first time exceeding the likely Domesday population, the majority
being resident in Cliddesden.[75] The population of Cliddesden parish rose gradually
from about 240 in 1801 (in 29 houses) to a peak of 334 in 1881 (in 70 houses), and
declined gradually from then until 1931, when it stood at 293 (in 76 houses). Two large
houses, Audleys Wood and Hackwood House with its park, contained approximately
one eighth of the population in 1891. The reduction in numbers which resulted from
the boundary changes in 1932 was small, since the areas mainly affected were in Hatch,
where the only houses at the time were Hatch Warren Farm and some farm cottages,
and on the Hackwood estate, where the tenant, an elderly widow, lived with a reduced
household.[76] Since 1932 both the population of Cliddesden and the number of houses
increased gradually. When the north-western boundary was moved to the M3 motorway
in 1985, Southlea was included in the parish for the first time. This was reflected in a
sharper intercensal increase than normal, from 386 in 1981 to 457 in 1991. In 2011 the
population of Cliddesden was 497 (in 205 dwellings).[77]

71   TNA, E 179/174/260, rot. 7d; E 179/174/272, rot. 7; *Hants Subsidy 1586*, 41.
72   *Hearth Tax*, 237.
73   TNA, E 179/176/569, rot. 7d; E 179/247/30, rot. 18.
74   *Dioc. Pop. Returns*, 490; *Compton Census*, 83.
75   *Parson and Parish*, 39, 267.
76   W.G. Atkin, *Hackwood* (priv. publ., 1945).
77   *Census*, 1981–2011.

LANDOWNERSHIP

IN 1086 CLIDDESDEN AND HATCH were separate manors, both in the hundred of Basingstoke. They were united under John de Valognes (I) in 1311. John Wallop (I), lord of Farleigh (d. 1486), acquired them and the subsequent descent of all three manors has been identical. John Wallop (III) was created earl of Portsmouth in 1743 and the family holdings are known as Portsmouth Estates.[1] Hatch retained its separate identity as a farm until the late 20th century. There have been changes in the parish and estate boundaries in the 20th and 21st centuries, but in 2017 Cliddesden was owned largely by Portsmouth Estates.

Cliddesden Manor and Estate

Before 1086 Cliddesden was held by two unnamed brothers, and afterwards by a certain Ralph Bloiet, with Durand of Gloucester as overlord.[2] Later overlords were stated to be Miles of Gloucester, 1st earl of Hereford, in the 12th century,[3] Reginald Fitz Peter in 1275,[4] and Matthew Fitz Herbert in 1339.[5] By 1486 at the latest, the overlords were the bailiffs of the borough of Basingstoke.[6]

The holders of the manor during the 12th century and much of the 13th century used 'of Cliddesden' as their surname. In 1167 Philip of Cliddesden accounted to the Exchequer for the manor and he was probably followed by Arnulf of Cliddesden (fl. 1167).[7] Next was Simon of Cliddesden, whose son William granted a half-hide to Nicholas, son of William of Swallick, in 1219.[8] William of Cliddesden was succeeded by John of Cliddesden, who also granted parts of the estate in 1252 and 1256, but in smaller quantities and for limited periods.[9] An earlier gift had been of 9 a. in c. 1240, which later became the property of the Hospital of St John in Basingstoke.[10]

1   *ODNB*, s.v. Wallop, John, first earl of Portsmouth (1690–1762), politician (accessed 23 Jan. 2017).
2   *Domesday*, 115. He held 11 manors, of Durand and of William, count of Eu: http://domesday.pase.ac.uk 'Ralph 86' (accessed 28 Jan. 2018).
3   *VCH Hants* IV, 145. No evidence has been found for this other than the presumed descent from Durand of Gloucester.
4   *Rot. Hund.* II, 221.
5   *Cal. Close* 1339–41, 153–4.
6   *Cal. Inq. p.m. Hen. VII*, I, no. 187.
7   *Pipe R* 1166–7 (PRS 11), 190; Dugdale, *Mon.* VII, 1014. He was recorded as a witness to an undated charter of Adam de Port at the end of the 12th century.
8   TNA, CP 25/1/203/4.
9   TNA, CP 25/1/204/9.
10 Baigent and Millard, *Basingstoke*, 601–2, 606.

John of Cliddesden sometimes used the name 'of Mattresdon',[11] derived from land he held in Matson, near Gloucester.[12] He was succeeded by his son Philip of Mattresdon.[13] By 1275, Cliddesden had passed to John's grandson, also called Philip of Mattresdon,[14] who kept and enlarged the family's Gloucestershire landholdings[15] and was rewarded for service in Wales in 1286.[16] By the beginning of the 14th century the manor and advowson of Cliddesden were both in the gift of Isabella, wife of William de Gardinis,[17] which implies that she had acquired them by inheritance, probably from the younger Philip of Mattresdon.[18] In 1303 she and her husband quitclaimed the manor and advowson to John de Berewyk,[19] who then passed them on as a gift to Ralph de Bereford.[20] Ralph resettled them, together with the manor and advowson of Hatch,[21] on John de Berewyk and John de Valognes (I) jointly in 1311, when the subsequent line of succession was set out in favour of John de Valognes (I) and his heirs, in the expectation that John de Berewyk, a churchman, would have none.[22] Both John de Berewyk and Ralph de Bereford were royal justices and administrators, who worked together for some years.[23] John de Berewyk had extensive landholdings in Hampshire, Surrey and Dorset, and held a number of valuable ecclesiastical livings. Neither of these men would have resided in Cliddesden, and John de Berewyk died in 1312, leaving John de Valognes (I) in sole possession of both manors.

The antecedents of John de Valognes (I) are not known, and neither is his relationship to the two royal justices. From 1311, the manors of Cliddesden and Hatch were united under the same lordship. Nicholas de Valognes held them in 1316[24] as did John de Valognes (II) in 1327.[25] He presented a rector to Cliddesden in 1333[26] but in 1337 he was convicted of having broken into a mill in Barton Stacey hundred belonging to the Prior of Southwick (Hants), and of having stolen a grindstone and a quantity of wheat. Since he was in minor orders, he was handed over to the jurisdiction of the bishop of Winchester, and imprisoned in Wolvesey Palace, where he died.[27] Cliddesden was taken into the king's hands, and granted to John Brocas,[28] but was restored to the convicted clerk's son, John de Valognes (III), in 1339.[29]

11   Ibid., 606.
12   *Excerpta e Rot. Finium* I, 457.
13   Ibid.
14   *Rot. Hund.* II, 221.
15   *VCH Glos.* IV, 440–1.
16   *Cal. Close* 1279–88, 392.
17   TNA, CP 25/1/205/15.
18   William de Gardinis also had land in Matson – *VCH Glos.* IV, 443.
19   TNA, CP 25/1/205/15.
20   TNA, CP 25/1/205/16.
21   Below – Hatch Manor.
22   TNA, CP 25/1/205/16.
23   *ODNB*, s.v. Berewyk, John (b. in or before 1252, d. 1312), justice; Bereford, Ralph (d. 1329), administrator and justice (accessed 23 Jan. 2017).
24   *Feudal Aids* II, 313.
25   TNA, E 179/173/4, rot. 5.
26   *Reg. Stratford* I, 431.
27   *Cal. Close* 1339–41, 153–4.
28   *Cal. Pat.* 1334–8, 488.
29   *Cal. Close* 1339–41, 153–4.

John de Valognes (III) was recorded as holding Cliddesden in 1346 and was still alive in 1373.[30] He was succeeded by Sir Nicholas de Valognes, who held the advowson of Cliddesden church in 1396[31] and was said to have been lord of both Cliddesden and Farleigh.[32] In 1428 Cliddesden was held by William Vachell,[33] probably through marriage to the daughter of Sir Nicholas de Valognes.[34] William Vachell was also lord of Farleigh, and alive in 1450,[35] but shortly afterwards he was replaced in both Cliddesden and Farleigh by John Wallop (I, d. 1486) from whose time Cliddesden and Hatch descended with Farleigh.[36]

Hatch Manor

The manor of Hatch was held before 1066 by Alsige, who may also have been the chamberlain who held Steventon. In 1086 Hatch was held by Geoffrey the chamberlain as a reward for services to the king's daughter Matilda, although his right was disputed by Oda of Winchester, a pre-Conquest thegn who claimed that Alsige had pledged Hatch to him by permission of the king himself.[37] It was held in 1167 by a certain Henry[38] but nothing else is known until the manor and advowson were granted, together with those of Cliddesden, to John de Berewyk and John de Valognes (I) in 1311. From that date the manor descended with Cliddesden and hence, from the mid 15th century, with Farleigh.

Other Estates

Land in the parish was not entirely held by the Wallop family. The part of Hackwood Park within the parish boundary was never in their hands, and neither was Pensdell Farm in the north of the parish, the owners of which are known from the mid 16th century onwards.[39] George Green of Weston Corbett owned scattered fields in Cliddesden in the 18th century, which formed the basis of a small part-owned, part-rented farm built up by William Spier in the 19th century.[40] Spier had retired by 1881 and his fields were amalgamated with those of neighbouring farms. The farmhouse belonging to Church Farm was let separately from the land from 1907 onwards and subsequently sold, and about half of its original acreage was sold in 1920 to the sitting tenant.[41] The remainder was incorporated into Pensdell Farm, which grew from 40 a. in 1842 to 287 a.

30 *Feudal Aids* II, 332; *Reg. Wykeham* I, 48.
31 *Reg. Wykeham* I, 201.
32 Below, Farleigh Wallop – Landownership.
33 *Feudal Aids* II, 344.
34 Below, Farleigh Wallop – Landownership.
35 Reg. Waynflete I, f. 10. William Vachell presented a rector to Farleigh church in 1450.
36 Reg. Waynflete I, f. 69. John Wallop presented a rector to Cliddesden church in 1454; below, Farleigh Wallop – Landownership.
37 *Domesday*, 120.
38 *Pipe R* 1166–7 (PRS 11), 189.
39 Below, Cliddesden – Social History.
40 HRO, 12M49/A15/6–7; 21M65/F7/53/1–2; *Census*, 1841–81.
41 *Census*, 1881; HRO, 15M84/3/1/1/56;15M84/3/1/12/7; TNA, MAF 32/972/61.

in 1941.[42] Most of the Pensdell land was bought by William Berry, 1st viscount Camrose in 1951 and transferred to the Hackwood Park Estate, but was sold again in 1997 to the Herriard Estate.[43]

Land ownership in Cliddesden has been more diverse than in Farleigh Wallop, but Portsmouth Estates was the major landholder in 2017.[44]

42   HRO, 10M57/E123; 21M65/F7/53/1–2; TNA, MAF 32/972/61.
43   HRO, 159M88/1231; 117M91/SP13; Chris Allen, pers. comm.
44   Below, Cliddesden – Economic History.

ECONOMIC HISTORY

Until the 20th century Cliddesden was an agricultural parish with the great majority of the population engaged on the land. Four of the five main farms were in the same manorial ownership – Church Farm and Manor Farm in the village, Hatch Warren, an outlying farm in the west and Swallick in the south-east. This was a prosperous farming community with sheep the main livestock on the chalk downlands and the chief crops being wheat, barley, roots and hay. Open fields existed in the 16th century but were no longer evident in 1786, having been informally enclosed over time. In contrast to the neighbouring parish of Farleigh Wallop, there was only a very small amount of woodland. Meadow was also limited and lay close to the houses in the village street. The village supported a few shops and the usual range of rural crafts and trades. Proximity to Basingstoke influenced trade and development. In the 21st century most residents worked outside the parish, commuting to Basingstoke and beyond.

The Agricultural Landscape

The late Anglo-Saxon settlement at Hatch belonged to a pattern of upland farms on Hampshire chalk downlands, and for a time survived the general shift towards the valleys. Cliddesden may be one of those valley settlements which developed from the 9th century onwards, as soil fertility on the chalk diminished and the introduction of the mouldboard plough enabled the heavier soil of the valleys to be worked.[1]

There is no evidence for the earliest open fields in Cliddesden, but in the late 16th century there were at least two large open fields as well as a number of smaller ones.[2] Some field names with 'mead' and 'croft' elements suggest that a certain amount of enclosure had already taken place. The largest open field was probably Rudgham in the south-east of the parish, a field which was subdivided into four parts by 1661.[3] A lease of 1677 refers to land 'lying dispersedly in the common fields of Cliddesden' and named five fields including Rudgham, and small relics of the fields remained in 1714.[4] Sheep-with-corn husbandry was then the mode of cultivation in the parish.

In 1841 the soil was described as a thin, flinty loam in the valleys and sides of the hills and chiefly clay on the higher ground, all on a chalk subsoil, and the total area of arable was 1,510 a. Meadow or pasture land amounted to 106 a., woodland to 183 a., glebe to just over 10 a. of meadow and waste to 15 a.[5] The rest of the meadow land was

1   Above, Cliddesden – Introduction; Banham and Faith, *Anglo-Saxon Farms*, 229–31.
2   HRO, 44M69/E5/2; below, Farleigh Wallop – Economic History.
3   Variants: Rudgiam, Ruddiham, Regems; HRO, 15M84/3/1/1/81.
4   HRO, 12M49/A15/2; 15M84/3/1/1/24.
5   TNA, IR 18/8949; HRO, 21M65/F7/53/1.

only found within Hackwood Park, and very small pieces of pasture lay behind or beside the houses on the Cliddesden street frontage. The woodland consisted of plantations in Hackwood Park and copses around Audleys Wood. Thirty years later, the acreages of arable and woodland were similar, at 1,580 a. and 157 a. respectively, but pasture had reduced to 46.5 a., the remaining acres having been classified as ornamental ground.[6] The arable field names, Great and Little Beggarwood, indicate woodland clearance before 1842 in Hatch, which was otherwise almost treeless.[7] In 2016 the agricultural landscape of Hatch, no longer in the parish, has been transformed by housing developments, and Hackwood Park is also outside the boundary. The agricultural landscape of Cliddesden itself is largely unchanged since the late 19th century.

Estate Management before 1600

In 1086 Cliddesden manor had land for five ploughteams (c.500–600 a.). The one-ploughland demesne farm was run by nine slaves and two tenant ploughs were shared among six villeins and ten bordars.[8] Contraction of the cultivated area is suggested by the disparity between the land for ploughteams and the number of ploughlands worked. No other land resources were listed. The value to the lord, including tenants' rents, was £3, a reduction from £4 before 1066. Hatch manor, under different lordship, had land for three ploughteams, of which two were in demesne and the third shared between two villeins. The demesne farm was worked by 11 slaves and no other land resources were listed. The value to the lord, including the villeins' rents, was £4, a reduction from £5 before 1066. The lordships of Cliddesden (including Hatch) and Farleigh were united in the 15th century and Farleigh House became the estate centre for all three manors.[9]

There are no records for estate management at Cliddesden and Hatch before 1580, but a well-established system was in place by the late 16th century. The evidence for Cliddesden and Hatch is the same as that for Farleigh Wallop, namely the accounts of Sir Henry Wallop (I).[10] A farm called 'Cliddesden farm' was leased, and there were a few freeholders and at least one copyholder, but some of the Cliddesden demesne was directly managed. Work on the demesne was done by a combination of paid employees, piece work and day labour. Some workers paid for their own food, others ate at the Farleigh farm as part of their wages, these variations perhaps reflecting earlier labour serices. The more fertile land, benefitting from better water supply and soils in the valley, was in Cliddesden and the majority of the demesne wheat, peas and vetches were grown on this part of the estate. Hatch, depopulated in the 14th century, was a sheep farm, with accommodation for a shepherd. It also contained a rabbit warren, leased to a warrener in 1580, who was expected to supply rabbits for the household at Farleigh House and elsewhere. There was no attempt at arable cultivation there in the late 16th century.

---

6 OS, *Book of Reference to the Plan of the Parish of Cliddesden* (1872).
7 HRO, 21M65/F7/53/1–2.
8 *Domesday*, 115.
9 Above, Cliddesden – Landownership.
10 HRO, 44M69/E5/1–5, 7; below, Farleigh Wallop – Economic History.

Tenant Farming before 1600

Knowledge of farming in the medieval period is largely gained from an understanding of similar parishes situated on the chalk downlands where flocks of sheep were run on the hills and arable crops, including corn and barley, were grown on lower land in the valley bottoms. Some late medieval tenant flocks were significant: in 1506, Richard Smyth of Cliddesden was fined for having 500 sheep on Basingstoke common.[11] Probate material from the 16th century shows that farming was mixed arable and pasture with sheep, the most important livestock, providing wool for the local cloth trade as well as meat and manure. The 17 surviving wills and 13 surviving inventories reveal a flourishing agricultural community. The total value of the inventories is £1,098, an average of £84 and range from £240 to £6.[12] The largest flock of sheep noted in 16th-century inventories was the 345 sheep on Francis Prince's farm in 1557, consisting of 181 wethers, four rams, 80 ewes and 80 lambs.[13] The flock had been built up from the 170 sheep left by his father, William, in 1544.[14] At Swallick Farm, a flock of 219 sheep made up of 94 wethers, 60 ewes and 65 tegs, was owned by Thomas Frye in 1596.[15] His son William (d. 1612) increased the flock to 280.[16] Thomas was the first known member of his family to farm at Swallick, a tradition that stretched for over 200 years; a William Frye was recorded there in 1777.[17] A smaller flock of 30 (1546) increased to 67 (1586),[18] a further illustration of the increase in flock numbers that demonstrate a pattern of growth throughout the 16th century. The mention of hurdles in two inventories suggests managed folding on the common fields.[19] Wheat was the main crop with 41 a. recorded on one farm in 1570.[20] There were only two crops of barley of any significant size – 36 a. (1549), and 17 a. (1574).[21] Other crops included oats, rye, vetches, peas and hay, intended for animal feed.

Whilst sheep were the main livestock, cattle were also kept, primarily for milk and milk products for which Basingstoke was an easily accessible market. In 1587–8 William Prince leased 22 cows and nine calves from the estate.[22] Other yeomen had eight cows and a bull or bullock, whilst five people had one cow each.[23] Cheeses, cheese vats and butter churns are recorded in several inventories.[24] Most testators kept pigs: the largest herd was that of Francis Prince consisting of 19 pigs, 10 hogs, one boar, 10 weaned pigs, one sow and four shoots (young pigs).[25] Flitches of bacon are found in five households,

---

11   Baigent and Millard, *Basingstoke*, 311.
12   Cliddesden probate material: https://www.victoriacountyhistory.ac.uk/explore/items/cliddesden-probate-material-1541-1560 (accessed 23 Jan. 2017).
13   HRO, 1557U/242.
14   HRO, 1544B/071.
15   HRO, 1596A/046.
16   HRO, 1612B/029.
17   HRO, 15M84/3/1/1/42.
18   HRO, 1559U/225; 1586A/93.
19   HRO, 1557U/242; 1574B/020.
20   HRO, 1570B/070.
21   HRO, 1549B/62; 1574B/020.
22   HRO, 44M69/E5/2.
23   Examples include HRO, 1576B/043; 1549B/62.
24   Examples include HRO, 1574B/020; 1588B/75.
25   HRO, 1557U/242.

one with 13 and another with 10 flitches respectively.[26] Tractive power was provided by horses – of the 37 horses listed in the surviving inventories, six appear to have been for riding; only one ox is recorded. Flocks of poultry included the usual hens, ducks and geese, but a mention of peacocks in 1549 and turkeys in 1570 appear to be fairly early references to such introductions to the country.[27] A widow, Joan King, had 37 stalls of bees, sufficient to supply honey for the village and perhaps further afield.[28] Others had one or two stalls each.

Estate Management 1600–1800

Nothing is known of estate management during the 17th century, but change is apparent by the early 18th century. The warren at Hatch was part of the marriage settlement of Alicia Wallop, and in 1712 her son John, later 1st earl of Portsmouth, obtained her consent to have the rabbits removed and the land converted to tillage.[29] All the Cliddesden open fields were enclosed by informal means by the late 18th century, and references in late 18th-century leases to additions and subtractions of fields when tenancies were transferred indicate that farms were being rationalised into fewer but larger units.[30] This was in line with the general trend on the Hampshire chalklands in the late 18th and early 19th centuries.[31] Annotations on the estate map of 1786 show the consolidated blocks of land assigned to the farmers of Church Farm, Manor Farm and Swallick Farm in the late 18th century.[32] Hatch was not surveyed in 1786, but a lease dated 1790 confirms that its lands were reorganised to include some adjacent fields in Farleigh Wallop.[33] This and other contemporary leases imposed strict conditions about sheep numbers to be folded and crops to be cultivated in a rotation of winter wheat, spring barley and two years of grass ley.

Tenant Farming 1600–1800

Only one inventory survives from the period of the Civil War but prosperity is shown to have continued from the 18 surviving wills and 14 surviving inventories dating from 1600 to 1684.[34] The inventories total £2,036, an average of £145 and range from £400 in 1676 to £15 in 1652.[35] Later indications of wealth are gained from bequests in wills.

26   HRO, 1596A/046; 1557U/242.
27   HRO, 1549B/62; 1570B/070.
28   HRO, 1576B/043.
29   HRO, 15M84/3/1/1/23.
30   HRO, 15M84/MP7; 15M84/3/1/1/35–6.
31   Bowie, 'Farming practices', 148–9.
32   HRO, 15M84/MP7; above, Cliddesden – Introduction.
33   HRO, 15M84/3/1/1/36.
34   Cliddesden probate material: https://www.victoriacountyhistory.ac.uk/explore/items/cliddesden-probate-material-1541-1560 (accessed 23 Jan. 2017).
35   HRO, 1676A/010; 1652A/41.

Henry Fry of Swallick Farm (d. 1730) left £800,[36] whilst John Dalman of Hatch (d. 1736) made bequests totalling £1,300.[37] It is not known how Dalman's assets were accumulated.

The open and enclosed fields which existed in the parish throughout the 17th century produced variable crop results. An example of the comparative worth of wheat grown on enclosed land with that in the common fields is provided in 1608 when 15 a. on Edward Austen's land was valued at £25 whilst 15½ a. of his crop in the common fields was valued at only £10.[38] Whilst the nature of soils may have varied, security and the opportunity to fertilise the land by grazing animals on it were obvious reasons for farmers to favour enclosure. In 1613 differences in outcomes between common fields in Cliddesden and Basingstoke are found when 13 a. of wheat grown in Cliddesden fields and 18 a. grown in Basingstoke fields were both valued at £12.[39]

In the late 17th century sheep continued to be the dominant livestock. Flocks of 275 and 150 sheep were owned by William Becke junior (d. 1676) and his father, also William (d. 1681).[40] Both were substantial farmers, the younger Becke having, in addition, 29 cattle and crops in the ground worth £181 10s. 0d. Barley and oats exceeded his acreage of wheat – the cultivation of barley increased in the parish from this time with the growth of a local malting industry.[41] Becke senior also owned a range and volume of equipment not found earlier: two dung carts, two ploughs, three pairs of harrows and two rollers, as well as five cart horses.

Sheep farming continued throughout the 18th century; a lease of Hatch farm in 1790 required 300 ewe sheep to be kept with their lambs, amounting to a flock of 600.[42] A 1798 schedule records only 935 sheep in the parish, an unexplained dip in numbers which returned to earlier levels by 1841.[43] Eight oxen are recorded in 1798, a change from the 16th century when horses appeared to have been the sole method of traction.

The practice of young, single farm workers living with the farmer in the farmhouse as 'servants in husbandry' was common.[44] However, annual hirings tied workers to their master, not always to the liking of either party. In 1786 a complaint was made by John Vickers of Hatch Warren against Charles Goodale, his servant in husbandry, for desertion. Goodale was committed to the bridewell at Odiham for one month.[45] In contrast, in 1779 Charles Hoar of Swallick Farm ordered Thomas Woolridge to leave his service and refused to pay for the month's work that Woolridge had completed. Woolridge's complaint was allowed and due wages ordered to be paid.[46]

36   HRO, 1730B/21.
37   TNA, PROB 11/675/207.
38   HRO, 1608A/005.
39   HRO, 1613B/03.
40   HRO, 1676A/010; 1681A/010.
41   Below, Cliddesden – Industry, Crafts, Commerce and Services.
42   HRO, 15M84/3/1/1/36.
43   HRO, Q22/1/2/5/3; TNA, IR 18/8949.
44   Kussmaul, *Servants*, passim.
45   HRO, 44M69/G3/661.
46   HRO, 44M69/G3/531.

Estate Management 1800–2016

Estate management policy for Cliddesden farms mirrored that of Farleigh Wallop throughout the 19th century.[47] Similar but even more demanding conditions than in earlier leases, incorporating root crops and separate fields of sainfoin, were imposed in 19th-century leases.[48] The terms of the leases were variable, usually between six and 14 years, although sometimes longer. Changes in policy were introduced in the early 1920s by Gerard Wallop, 9th earl of Portsmouth from 1943. He was a noted agricultural expert, who had managed the Hampshire family estates in person since 1923 before succeeding to the earldom.[49] He concentrated his work on the Farleigh estate, and permitted the remaining Portsmouth farms in Cliddesden and Hatch to be leased on long tenancies, although this meant some loss of control over their farming regimes. The earl transferred his farming interests to Kenya in 1950, and left the Hampshire estates to be managed by trustees. Swallick Farm was sold in 1951 and added to the Hackwood estate.[50] The earl's grandson, Quentin, the 10th earl of Portsmouth, assumed personal control of his Hampshire estates in the 1970s and took Manor Farm in hand although the farmhouse continued to be rented out. He also farmed the land of Swallick Farm as a leaseholder from 1999 until 2007, and most of that area was subsequently bought back by Portsmouth Estates. Land at Church Farm, sold in 1920, was also bought back by Portsmouth Estates in 2015, consolidating the core of the estate.[51]

Farming 1800–2016

Livestock and Crops

Sheep farming on the downland continued until the early 21st century with peaks and troughs. In 1841 there were 1,300 ewes and their lambs, valued at £780, and 650 tegs whose fleeces were valued at £307. In 1870 sheep numbers were 2,223 but then fell dramatically to 1,222 in 1891, 992 in 1911 and 476 in 1931 during the prolonged agricultural depression that started in the late 1870s and affected arable-based mixed farming systems as farmers competed with cheap imports of wheat, wool and, after 1900, refrigerated lamb. During the Second World War arable farming necessarily took precedence and in 1951 the total number of sheep recorded was only 51.[52] A resurgence in sheep farming in the parish led to an increase in numbers to 503 sheep in 1971, 930

---

47   Below, Farleigh Wallop – Economic History.
48   HRO, 15M84/3/1/1/50–1; 15M84/E6/1/24.
49   Below, Farleigh Wallop – Economic History.
50   HRO, 15M84/2/1/6/11.
51   Greta Iddeson, Estate Manager, pers. comm., 2016.
52   TNA, MAF 68/4349/61.

Figure 15 *Ploughing with horses at Manor Farm c.1947.*

in 1981 and 1,402 in 1988.[53] The eventual demise of sheep farming came in 2004; it was economically no longer viable.[54]

By contrast there were only 15 cows in 1841. Numbers of cattle slowly increased from 44 in 1870 to 267 in 1931 and the number of pigs kept also increased from 96 to 311 in the same period.[55] Cattle and pigs had ceased to be farmed by the mid-1980s.[56] Horses engaged in agriculture reached a height with 127 in 1891.[57]

Arable crops occupied most land in the parish in 1841 (1510 a. of 1824 a. total) with 300 a. of wheat valued at £2,100 and 300 a. of barley at £1,680. Fodder crops included clover and sainfoin, tares and rye, grass and turnips. A four-field 'shift' was practised, turnips, barley, seeds and wheat on the lower ground and bare fallow, wheat, oats and seeds on the higher ground.[58] Husbandry was deemed 'of average' for the neighbourhood but farmers were urged to find a better way of converting their straw into manure, allegedly a serious defect throughout the district. Arable crops remained relatively stable with around 300–400 a. of wheat and 100–180 a. of barley grown annually between 1870 and 1931 but fodder crops were marked by increases in turnips (309 a. in 1870) as was the percentage of clover sown amongst grasses.[59]

Market gardening benefitted from the proximity of Basingstoke and good transport links to London. A nursery started by the Miller family on Station Road in the 1930s had glass houses on 3 a. of land and grew lettuce, cucumbers and other horticultural crops, sold at their market stall in Basingstoke. The business had a new owner in 1984

53   TNA, MAF 68/5224/61; MAF 68/5750/61; MAF 68/6108/61.
54   Chris Allen, pers. comm., 2017.
55   TNA, MAF 68/242/61; MAF 68/1325/61; MAF 68/2465/61; MAF 68/3566/61.
56   Ken Rampton, pers. comm., 2017.
57   TNA, MAF 68/1325/61.
58   TNA, IR 18/8949. The terms of the leases at this time actually imply a five-course rotation.
59   TNA, MAF 68/1325/61.

Figure 16 *Dinner break during the harvest at Hatch Warren Farm c.1905. Back row left to right, Johnny Wyeth aged c.71 retired carter, Frederick Wyeth 2nd carter, Harry Martin labourer,? Goodall under-carter, two lads driving the horses, Dave Hedges under-carter, William Hayward head carter, Eli Bowman head under-carter, Bill Buckland under-carter. Front row left to right, two boys leading horses, three younger boys who have come to watch and play.*

but did not survive the damage caused by the great storm of 1987.[60] Soft fruit was grown on the field behind Southlea and strawberries were supplied to the Wimbledon tennis championships from 1951 for five or six years. The fruit was picked, packed and transported by road each morning.[61] In 1990 a 'pick your own' scheme operated at this site.[62]

Farms and Agricultural Workers

A comparison of occupations between 1851 and 1901 shows that agriculturally linked jobs remained predominant. In 1851 of a population of 314, there were five farmers, 61 agricultural labourers and 10 shepherds, including five boys. Fifty years later, when the population was only marginally higher at 321, there were two farmers and a farm bailiff, 21 farm carters, 24 farm labourers, four shepherds and a gamekeeper.[63]

Resident farm servants continued to be hired throughout England for much of the 19th century but the practice dwindled as labour became more available and farmers struggled to compete with cheap food imports from abroad.[64] Francis Budd, at Hatch Warren, had seven carter boys aged 14–20 years living in the farm house in 1861. In 1891 an under-shepherd and two carter boys aged 16–18 were similarly housed and employed, an unusually late example of service in husbandry.[65] As in earlier times, occasional friction between servants and master occurred. Three men deserted the service of Mr

60   TNA, MAF 68/3566/61; Ken Rampton pers. comm., 2017; *Cliddesden Village Newsletter*, Jul. 1984.
61   TNA, MAF 68/4349/61; Ken Rampton pers. comm., 2017.
62   *Cliddesden Village Newsletter*, Feb. 1990.
63   *Census*, 1851, 1901. The reduced number of farmers in 1901 may reflect the absence or non-residence of farmers on the census day.
64   Kussmaul, *Servants*, passim.
65   *Census*, 1861, 1891.

Figure 17 *William Hayward, head carter Hatch Warren Farm c.1900, at the top of Kempshott hill with an early 4 foot, 2 horse McCormick binder.*

Budd in 1859 and each was fined 10s. and two others absconded in 1868. The latter were made to complete their contracts and were fined for their offence.[66] No evidence of the custom has been found in Cliddesden after 1891.

A photograph of men and boys at Hatch Warren Farm in c.1905 illustrates farming life in Cliddesden at the beginning of the 20th century, the work dependent on horse power and manual labour. A hierarchy existed within the group from boy to head carter, responsibilities and status increasing with age and skill. Family links also bound the workers together.[67]

Mechanisation slowly made its way on to the farms. A McCormick binder at Hatch Warren Farm was in use about 1900; later binders were 6 ft wide and pulled by three horses. By 1941 Manor Farm had two International tractors and Pensdell had a Fordson but in 1951 there were still 15 horses engaged in agriculture in the parish. Horses had gone by the 1960s, replaced by motor power – at Manor Farm this included a Ferguson T20 and later a Ferguson diesel 45hp tractor.[68]

Consolidation of farms began when John William Hooper took the tenancy of Manor Farm in 1904 and two years later added the tenancy of Church Farm, forming a block of land in the western half of the parish.[69] Ernest Hooper succeeded his father and in 1949 established a milking parlour and dairy at Manor Farm.[70] In 1978 the farms were split. Manor Farm became part of the land farmed by the 10th earl of Portsmouth while Richard Hooper continued at Church Farm on the land his family had bought in 1920, with additional land purchased in 1981.[71] Poultry were kept until the early 1980s and cattle until the mid-1980s; from then on it was a largely arable farm.[72]

---

66   *Hants Telegraph and Sussex Chron.*, 9 Jul. 1859, 28 Jul. 1868.
67   For example, Frederick Wyeth, 2nd carter, married head carter William Hayward's daughter – Edward Roberts, pers. comm., 2014.
68   Ken Rampton, pers. comm., 2016.
69   TNA, MAF 32/972/61.
70   HRO, 15M84/E6/4/67.
71   Below, Cliddesden – Social History.
72   Ken Rampton, pers. comm., 2016.

Change took place at Swallick Farm when a new tenant, Eric Seldon, arrived in 1943 and took over what had been a failing farm,[73] remaining at Swallick for over 50 years. He ran a mixed farm of 401 a. rented at £1 an acre, with 30 cows, hand-milked, and first-year lambs brought down from Scotland to be reared. Pigs and a bull were kept. During the Second World War, Land Army girls worked on the farm and the walled garden was hand-dug for vegetables. In 1993 Swallick was an arable farm, with a reduced acreage. Farm buildings included four barns, a granary and cart shed, some of which were rented out.[74]

At Pensdell Farm, Edward Clift was the tenant in 1941, his family having farmed at Pensdell since at least 1859.[75] He farmed 287 a. with a labour force of five men and two women and kept 69 cattle, 176 sheep and 110 poultry as well as wheat, barley, oats, mixed corn, potatoes, mangolds, kale, clover/sainfoin, grass and 10 tons of straw.[76] From 1997 it was farmed by a tenant of the Herriard Estate.[77] Other smaller holdings included Hill View Farm, 73 a., part-owned, part-rented by Henry Lay in 1941 where he kept Hampshire Down sheep and crops included wheat, barley, oats and mustard. There was also a poultry farm in Hackwood Lane at this time.[78]

In 2016 one tenant farmer, Chris Allen of Farleigh Wallop, became responsible for all the farm land in Cliddesden owned by the estate. His workforce, which covered both Cliddesden and Farleigh Wallop, consisted of five men, two cowmen and a woodman.[79] The farm land throughout the parish was devoted to arable crops with small pastures used for grazing by horses kept for leisure purposes. No farmhouses, used as such, remained; all had been sold or let away from agriculture.

Industry, Crafts, Commerce and Services

The Cloth Industry

By the early 16th century Basingstoke had a thriving cloth industry which was a major factor in its prosperity. The town was ranked 51st in the country by wealth in 1524–5.[80] Basingstoke and its hinterland were linked through the production of wool and its manufacture. Cliddesden was part of that wider industrial hinterland with successful clothiers such as John Belchamber migrating there in the early 16th century and farmers combining agriculture with the cloth trade.[81]

---

73   TNA, MAF 32/977/66. Swallick Farm was included with Farleigh Wallop returns.
74   HRO, 64M99/B254.
75   *White's Dir.*, 1859.
76   TNA, MAF 32/972/61.
77   Chris Allen, pers. comm., 2016.
78   TNA, MAF 32/972/61.
79   Chris Allen, pers. comm., 2016.
80   A. Dyer, 'Ranking list of English medieval towns' in D.M. Palliser (ed.), *The Cambridge Urban History of Britain i* (Cambridge, 2000), 766; J. Hare, 'Church-building and urban prosperity on the eve of the Reformation: Basingstoke and its parish church', *Proc. Hants F.C. 62* (2007), 185–97.
81   Below, Cliddesden – Social History.

Thomas Walker, also a clothier, moved from Basingstoke to Pensdell Farm, Cliddesden, on his marriage to John Belchamber's widow, assuming responsibility for the farm as well as carrying on the cloth business there. At his death in 1549 Walker had quantities of wool, tools and cloth in his shop at 'Penns'. The value of wool is given in his inventory: 29 tods of white wool in the fleece worth £30; seven tods of white wool worth £9; one tod of blue wool valued at £1 10s. 0d.; 14 lbs of white yarn worth 14s. and 12 lbs watchet leaving valued at 12s.; a total of £51 16s. 0d. His tools included six pairs of shears, a pair of pairing shears, two scraws and 10 burling irons for final finishing of the cloth. Along with two great old wool bags were various types of flock – 'draughts' and 'sheers' – and amongst his debts were sums for teasels, dyeing and for the sealing of kerseys.[82]

Testamentary evidence suggests an active cloth industry with tenant farmers such as Francis Prince (d. 1557), Thomas Blundell (d. 1574) and Thomas Frye (d. 1596) each with one or two spinning wheels and two or three sheep shears, and Blundell and Frye with 16 lbs of wool and 20 lbs of lambswool, respectively. In 1643, Thomas Belchamber – the family continued at Pensdell after Walker's death – was still in the cloth business, his inventory recorded: 'For wool money received, £4 11s. 9d.'[83]

Three linen wheels are recorded in 1612–13 whilst only three spinning wheels appear in inventories for the whole century, changes suggesting a decline in the industry. The price of wool had fallen from its height in the 1540s to that obtained in the 1670s when, for example, 18 tods of wool were valued at only £11 14s. 0d. Nevertheless, William Becke was still described as a 'farmer and clothier' in a lease of 1692.[84]

Malting and Brewing

Small-scale commercial brewing was common in medieval households, and during the 14th and 15th centuries Cliddesden residents were occasionally fined at the Basingstoke views of frankpledge for breaches of the assize of ale.[85] In the 16th century three farmers had malt houses in their yards and evidence of malting and brewing exists throughout the following century.[86] Malting grew in importance as the wool industry declined and by 1819 a commercial malt house existed in Cliddesden.[87] In 1835 Henry Cobden is recorded as a maltster.[88] At the sale of the malt house in 1883 it was described as a two-storey malt house with a malt kiln with furnace, a leaded cistern, an excellent barley granary and malt stores. A dwelling house was adjacent with orchard, meadow and outbuildings including a brewery and a small cottage – suggesting that there was sufficient work for two people. The property of about 3 a., with a frontage of 54 yd. on the main village street, was let to George Thorp, 'an elderly tenant', at £25 a year.[89] As well as serving its own brewery, it was well-placed to supply malt to breweries in Basingstoke.

82   HRO, 1549B/62.
83   Cliddesden probate material: https://www.victoriacountyhistory.ac.uk/explore/items/cliddesden-probate-material-1541-1560 (accessed 23 Jan. 2017).
84   HRO, 15M84/3/1/1/21.
85   HRO, 148M71/2/1/1–64.
86   Examples include HRO, 1557U/242; 1586A/93.
87   HRO, 11M94/21: it was owned by Merton College, Oxford, and sold to Richard Curtis of Basingstoke in Jan. 1819.
88   HRO, 1835A/099.
89   HRO, 10M57/SP356.

Smiths and Other Crafts

Cliddesden had two blacksmiths' forges, the first at Pryers Park (Priory Pick) adjacent to Manor Farm where Ambrose Dawman lived and had his smithy in the early 17th century and where William Cox and his son, Jesse, were smiths in the early 19th century.[90] The other forge was attached to the Old School House, and is probably where George Slater was blacksmith in 1871.[91] A wheelwright, Henry Tilbery, worked in the village in 1730.[92] Thomas Switsur was a wheelwright in 1816 as was John Switsur in 1859, the family living and working at Bowling Alley until 1876.[93] Demand for wheelwrights was high in the second half of the 19th century and there were sometimes two in the village.[94] Richard Waldren worked as a shoemaker for over 40 years from 1835; his shoe shop is recorded in 1861.[95] There was a boot maker, Charles Felstone, working in Cliddesden in 1935.[96]

Milling

Without a river in the parish, farmers may have taken their grain to a windmill at Farleigh Wallop to have it ground.[97] Alternatively, water mills on the river Loddon such as Eastrop Mill or Upper Mill, close to Black Dam in Basingstoke, or any of the three mills in Basing were all accessible.[98]

Commerce and Services

In 1851 Cliddesden had a grocer's shop run by William Roberts;[99] his daughter ran the shop in 1898.[100] A post office opened in 1846 but may have closed and re-opened; the first postmistress to be shown in census returns is in 1881.[101] Mrs Margaret Hutchins was the sub-postmistress in 1911 at which time there were two postal deliveries and collections a day and it provided a money order service and telegraph office.[102] In 1936 a shop and post office opened on the premises which had previously belonged to Thorntons of Basingstoke and which had been used as a bakery.[103] The business closed in 1997 and the post office was replaced for a temporary period by a travelling post office.[104]

90   HRO, 1637A/025; 15M84/2/1/6/2; 1834A/23.
91   Below, Cliddesden – Social History; *Census*, 1871.
92   HRO, 20M51/74.
93   HRO, 10M57/SP15; 1835A/099; 5M62/15/448; 15M84/2/1/6/4.
94   *White's Dir.*, 1859–78.
95   HRO, 1835A/099; *Census*, 1861.
96   *Kelly's Basingstoke Dir.*, 1935.
97   Below, Farleigh Wallop – Economic History.
98   A. Vaidya (ed.), *The Mills and Millers of Hampshire*, 3 vols (Hampshire Mills Group, 2011–13), III, passim.
99   *Census*, 1851.
100 *Kelly's Dir. Hants.*, 1898.
101 www.sites.google.com/site/ukpostofficesbycounty: post offices of England (accessed 17 Mar. 2016); *Census*, 1851–81.
102 *Kelly's Dir. Hants.*, 1911.
103 *Basingstoke Gaz.*, 19 Sept. 2003. Henry Thornton, grocer, was recorded in *Kelly's Dir. Hants.*, 1903.
104 *Cliddesden Village Newsletter*, June/July 1998.

Figure 18 *The Jolly Farmer, showing the doors of the three original cottages.*

In 2016 a kite and banner maker operated from the original Methodist chapel and there was a small pottery painting studio in the old shop building.

A number of men were employed in the construction of the Basingstoke and Alton Light Railway and also as station staff once the line opened in 1901.[105] Unusually for a village, a gas main was laid to Cliddesden in 1923 and a supply was connected to 33 houses. In the following year three street lights were installed.[106] In the early 1900s Tom Mansbridge came to the village and opened a cycle engineer's shop, which was to become a garage. His son, Bill Mansbridge ran the school bus service for 49 years until his death in 1978.[107] The garage was still operating in 2016, as was a garage specialising in Volvo vehicles established in redundant farm buildings at Pensdell Farm in 1991.[108]

Public Houses

The first known public house in Cliddesden was the Jolly Farmer on Farleigh Road which began life as a retail beer house in the 1840s and became an alehouse in 1868 when John Sparsholt, a blacksmith as well as publican, was granted a full licence, enabling him to sell wine and spirits as well as beer.[109] Held on lease from Merton College, Oxford, by Richard Curtis of Basingstoke, at an auction in 1850 it was described thus:

> A roomy and substantially built brick and tile dwelling house, now divided in three tenements, the centre used as a retail beer house, The Jolly Farmer, with

105 Above, Cliddesden – Introduction.
106 HRO, 19M65/B67: the company was the Basingstoke Gas and Coke Co. We are indebted to Joan Wilson for this reference.
107 *Basingstoke Gaz.*, 20 Jan. 1978; *Kelly's Dir. Hants.*, 1911.
108 www.garagebasingstoke.co.uk/index.php/volvo-warranty/about-us (accessed 18 Mar. 2016).
109 HRO, 10M57/SP70; 10M57/O2/22; *Hampshire Advertiser*, 5 Sept. 1868.

large tap room, parlour, brew house, 4 bed rooms and attics. Two cellars, and
large gardens; also a yard, barn, piggery and about 1a. 3 r. 2 p. of good arable
land … and is now in the occupation of John Harfield.[110]

In 1872 the owner was John May, a Basingstoke brewer, and in February 1950 John
May & Co, sold it to H. & G. Simonds.[111] Simonds Brewery was acquired by Courage,
Barclay and Co. Ltd. in 1960.[112] Operating as a free house, the Jolly Farmer was the only
public house in the village in 2017, serving food and drink and attracting visitors from
Basingstoke and beyond.

The Three Horseshoes was a public house situated in Woods Lane in an area known
as Coldharbour. William Switsur was a beer retailer there in 1901 and appears to have
remained as landlord until his death in 1920 at the age of 91.[113] Switsur and his wife Sarah
(d. 1902) had been the innkeeper and landlady at the Jolly Farmer in 1881 before moving
around the corner to the Three Horseshoes.[114] Whilst geographically very close, the two
public houses were in different licensing authorities, the Basingstoke boundary dividing
them.[115] Opening hours varied between the two, an advantage enjoyed by residents.[116]
Originally owned by Farnham United Breweries, the Three Horseshoes was bought by
Courage Brewery in the 1950s.[117] It closed in the 1970s and returned to being a private
residence.

Commercial Developments since 1990

Portsmouth Estates introduced a policy of diversification in the late 20th century.
The redundant agricultural buildings at Manor Farm were the first on the estate to be
converted from agricultural use to office/commercial use in the early 1990s.[118] In 1992 a
children's day nursery was created in what had been a dairy building.[119] Richard Hooper
of Church Farm restored the black barn, originally used for grain drying and storage, and
converted it to commercial units. The work was completed in 2002 when it was handed
over to new owners.[120] In 2016 there were also livery stables, a canine hydrotherapy
centre and a number of small home-based businesses.

---

110 HRO, 10M57/SP70.
111 HRO, 97M83/XP140.
112 www.breweryhistory.com/Breweries/BerksReadingSimonds (accessed 27 Dec. 2016).
113 *Census*, 1901; *Kelly's Dir. Hants.*, 1907; HRO, 31M82/PR9.
114 *Census*, 1881–1901.
115 HRO, 97M83/XP143; 77M82/XP47.
116 *Basingstoke Gaz.*, 14 Jul. 1978.
117 HRO, 77M82/XP47.
118 www.hollishockley.co.uk: news item 12 Sept. 2011 (accessed 4 Jan. 2016).
119 Below, Cliddesden – Social History.
120 *Cliddesden Village Newsletter*, May 2002, 10.

LANDSCAPE AND GEOGRAPHICAL LOCATION HAVE influenced the pattern of life in Cliddesden. A farming community from the Middle Ages, the village developed along the sides and bottom of a dry valley in the chalk downlands, centred around the staggered crossroads and the focal meeting point of the pond. The compact nature of the settlement doubtless helped community cohesion. Migration from Basingstoke, only two miles distant, has taken place from the 16th century if not earlier, as individuals became affluent and sought a rural lifestyle whilst still within easy travelling distance of the town's facilities. Others moved from the village into the town to pursue trading opportunities. A school established in 1656 was an unusually early example of educational provision in the rural villages around Basingstoke. Charitable help for the school and for relief of the poor was extensive; members of the Wallop family and many of the clergy were generous donors.

The 20th century saw great societal change shifting from an agricultural community to one which, after 1950, included many incoming professional and managerial residents as well as retirees from Basingstoke and elsewhere. The last shop, which also provided a post office, closed in 1997 but the church, the school, the village hall and the public house flourished in 2016.

Social Structure and Character

The Middle Ages

In the 14th century the recorded population of Cliddesden was of average size for the rural settlements around Basingstoke. Tenant families of greater importance than their peers may have included that of the two John le Loquers, elder and younger, assessed to pay the highest taxes of ten contributors in 1327.[1] Some members of the family moved to Basingstoke, where they prospered in the 14th and 15th centuries.[2] The impact of the Black Death on Cliddesden is difficult to evaluate. Five rectors succeeded each other during the years 1348–9, the high turnover presumed to be a consequence of the plague.[3] The community, however, did not suffer the devastating decline of its neighbours, its survival no doubt at the expense of Hatch and Farleigh Wallop, and may well have

1   *Hants Tax 1327*, 20. Later variants of the name included Loker, Locker, Lowker and Louker.
2   J. Hare, *Basingstoke: A Medieval Town, c.1000–c.1600* (2017), 56, 70.
3   Below, Cliddesden – Religious History.

Figure 19 *Cliddesden pond c.1928.*

benefitted from rising prices, greater availability of land and from the growing cloth industry in the area.

16th–18th Centuries

Cliddesden continued to thrive. In a tax assessment of 1525 it had more people with goods valued at higher levels and fewer people assessed to pay the lowest rate than those in adjacent parishes.[4] Prominent residents included the Prince and Belchamber families. William Prince (d. 1544) and Francis Prince (d. 1557) were prosperous sheep farmers, on good terms with the Wallop family, lords of the manor. Oliver Wallop was one of the overseers of Francis Prince's will and was given the 'best boar' for his pains; Lady Wallop gave John, son of Francis, a gold chain at his christening.[5] John Belchamber (d. 1546) had bought Pensdell Farm in the early 16th century.[6] His widow Matilda was probably the wealthiest inhabitant of the parish, heading the tax lists of 1546 and 1547 and married Thomas Walker, a Basingstoke clothier (d. 1549).[7] Walker left 6s. 8d. to Cliddesden church, asking to be buried within it – a privilege usually retained for the gentry. His house consisted of a hall, pantry, parlour, loft over the parlour, loft over the hall, kitchen,

---

4   TNA, E 179/173/183, rot. 5.
5   HRO, 1544B/071; HRO, 1557U/242.
6   J. Hare, 'Inns, innkeepers and the society of late medieval England, 1350–1600', *Jnl of Medieval Hist.* 39 (2013), 493; HRO, 1546B/016.
7   TNA, E 179/174/260, rot. 7d; E 179/174/272, rot. 7.

yealing house, shop (tool store) and haystore.[8] Five generations of the Belchamber family remained in Cliddesden. The aspiration of Thomas (d. 1600) that 'my lands should continue and be amongst the name of Belchamber of my own blood and issue' was fulfilled until at least 1677, when John Belchamber of Cliddesden was recorded as a party to a land transaction.[9]

The parish hierarchy can be determined by an analysis of the hearth tax returns and probate records of the 17th century. Cliddesden had 26 households recorded in the 1665 hearth tax assessment, sixth most populous of the 14 outer Basingstoke parishes.[10] The rector, Edward Mooring (d. 1673), had the largest house with seven hearths.[11] In his will he left a silver tankard, flaxen sheets, Turkey work carpets and lands in Stoke and Hurstbourne Priors.[12] Amongst the leading families in 1665 were tenant yeomen William Becke, William Prince and John Kersley, all with substantial houses each with five hearths.[13] William Becke (d. 1681) farmed 120 a., leased from Henry Wallop.[14] His goods, valued at £310 10s. 6d., included leather chairs, leather stools and large amounts of linen.

The middling rank of village society was probably represented by the five families who, in 1665, were living in houses with three or four hearths. Included in this group were Henry Barrett, yeoman (d. 1673), whose inventory included 63 ewes and tegs, 12½ a. of wheat and total goods valued at £100 9s. 0d.,[15] and John Belchamber at Pensdell.[16] The number and proportion of those deemed poor are indicated by the householders excused payment of the hearth tax. Five of 26 householders were excused payment in 1665, two of whom were widows.[17] Six of 23 householders were not chargeable in 1673,[18] and seven of 26 householders were excluded in 1675.[19] The labouring poor, around one quarter of the population, was lower than the average at the time and in the neighbourhood.[20]

Household possessions were another indicator of status as furniture became more plentiful and more comfortable in the 17th century. An inventory of 1643 included a great chest, a court cupboard, three tables, five chairs, three feather beds, a cradle, carpet and cushions.[21] By the end of the century signs of gentility could be found. John Chisul (d. 1678), rector, had books and a clock,[22] whilst the 1681 inventory of William Becke,

8   HRO, 1549B/62.
9   TNA, PROB 11/96/39; HRO, 12M49/A15/2.
10   *Hearth Tax*, 237.
11   Ibid.
12   TNA, PROB 11/343/217.
13   *Hearth Tax*, 237.
14   HRO, 1681A/010.
15   HRO, 1673AD/005.
16   *Hearth Tax*, 237.
17   Ibid.
18   TNA, E 179/176/569, rot. 7d.
19   TNA, E 179/247/30, rot. 18.
20   For example, Mapledurwell with the same number of chargeable households in 1665 had 15 non-chargeable households compared with Cliddesden's five.
21   HRO, 1643AD/06.
22   HRO, 1678AD/030.

yeoman, included 'books in and about the home' and 'an old clock'.[23] A century later, in 1788, Mary Rowell owned a watch – an unusual and valuable object.[24]

An increasing disparity between rich and poor is evident as the 18th century progressed. Whilst people had been bound together through common endeavours in working the land, a widening of social backgrounds and occupations in the parish led to divisions. A gentleman such as Thomas Savage (d. 1751) who held lands in Basingstoke, including Hound Mill, represented a new strand in the social structure.[25] His widow Susannah drew attention to her status with directions in her will that a stone be erected above her grave in Cliddesden churchyard and that six poor men carry her to her grave.[26] Other parishioners were prospering as they dealt in land and property.[27] Wills show the importance attached to keeping property and money within families; a number of examples exist of the disinheritance of widows on the day of their remarriage.[28] In the same period, the poor had lives of a very different order – incidents in the 1780s of petty stealing of turnips or hedgewood being indicative of their situation.[29]

1800–2016

The Swing Riots

In November 1830 a wave of rural protest, known as the Swing Riots, swept across much of southern England. Opposition to labour-displacing threshing machines was one expression of discontent that included wage levels, tithe and rent payments and inadequate poor law allowances. John Gold and William Astridge from Cliddesden were spokesmen for a 'mob' of around 50 labourers who visited Down Grange in Basingstoke on 19 November. Negotiations were peaceable, unlike events that took place the following week when a band of men revisited Down Grange as well as Wootton St Lawrence and Monk Sherborne. A threshing machine was broken at Down Grange and one at Monk Sherborne was destroyed by a farmer before the mob reached him. Four men from Cliddesden, Charles and John Bulpitt, George Clarke and James Cook stood trial before the Special Commission held in Winchester on December 20th. Charged with unlawful assembly, riot and disturbance and with stealing two sovereigns and one half sovereign, 'given' them by terrified landowners, they were all sentenced to death, later commuted to transportation. They sailed on the *Eleanor* for New South Wales and their convict indents reveal their trades and education: two of them ploughed, reaped and sowed and one of these also milked, one was a bricklayer's labourer and one a carter; two could read and write.[30] No farms were visited in Cliddesden. Farleigh Wallop also escaped the rioters' attentions. Such tumultuous events must, however, have impinged on relationships between the landlord, tenant farmers and their workforce in this small community.

23   HRO, 1681A/010.
24   HRO, 1788A/080.
25   TNA, PROB 11/787/53. Houndmills became an industrial area of the modern town.
26   HRO, 1767A/090.
27   HRO, 1774A/027; 1786A/29.
28   HRO, 1732A/058; TNA, PROB 11/787/53; HRO, 1774A/027; 1781B/24.
29   HRO, 44M69/G3/645, 699.
30   Chambers, *Rebels*, 137–8, 155, 157.

The Life of the Community

Crime was usually of a low order with occasional incidents of stealing and game offences.[31] Serious offences included an indecent assault on a little girl by a boy aged 14, and an 'unnatural crime', not specified, resulting in four months imprisonment with hard labour and a year's imprisonment in Winchester gaol respectively.[32] In December 1888 three youths aged 17, 14 and 12 were indicted for burglary and stealing 3 lbs lard and other articles valued at 5s. 8d. They admitted guilt and were sentenced to nine months, six months and one month imprisonment each, all with hard labour; severe punishment for youthful offenders.[33]

Changes to the very settled community can be seen as the 19th century progressed. In 1851, whereas 194 people, of a population of 314, were born in the parish and 84 were born in Hampshire, by 1901, when the population had risen slightly to 324, those figures had become 78 and 163 respectively. In 1901, 83 people had been born outside Hampshire, some from as far afield as Newcastle-upon-Tyne, London and Tiverton, and one birthplace was in Bombay.[34]

John Bird, a Leader in Local Society

John Bird (1845–1905) was an astute business man and a staunch Methodist, two aspects of his life which underlay his contribution to parish society. Bird had come to Basingstoke in 1877 where, with his brother, he had established the *Hants and Berks. Gazette*, the first newspaper to be printed in the town. In 1884 he moved to Cliddesden, living at Farleigh Dene, a substantial house in the village street.[35]

At Cliddesden, John Bird represented the parish on the Board of Guardians and Rural District Council for about 15 years. He was also chairman of the Cliddesden school board and, after 1903, a manager of the Cliddesden council school. Bird was chairman of Cliddesden parish council from 1896 and acted as a trustee and secretary of the Cliddesden and Farleigh Wallop parochial charities. It was in these two roles that he called upon the Charity Commission to investigate the complicated history of benefactions to the parish and succeeded in re-establishing yearly payments of the school endowment as well as ensuring that a proper scheme was drawn up for the charities' administration.[36] He was, in addition, the chairman of the Cliddesden branch of the Hampshire and General Friendly Society.[37]

On coming to Basingstoke, John Bird had allied himself with the then newly-established Wesleyan Methodist cause and he was a local preacher for many years. It was largely due to Bird's instigation and drive that a redundant Methodist chapel in Basingstoke was removed stone by stone and rebuilt in Southlea, providing Cliddesden with a much larger and more spacious building than the original small chapel on the opposite side of Farleigh road.[38]

31 Examples include HRO, 44M69/G3/645; *Hants Advertiser*, 7 Jan. 1871.
32 *Hants Advertiser*, 17 Jun. 1871, 21 Feb. 1877.
33 *Hants Telegraph and Sussex Chron.*, 15 Dec. 1888.
34 *Census*, 1851, 1901.
35 www.basingstokegazette.co.uk/aboutus (accessed 3 Jan. 2015).
36 Below, Cliddesden – Charities.
37 *Hants and Berks. Gaz.*, 28 Jan. 1905.
38 Below, Cliddesden – Religious History.

Farming Families

Farming families played important roles in village society, amongst them the Clift family in the 19th century and the early 20th century. Norman Clift was a member of the school board[39] and Daniel Clift was an assistant overseer and clerk of the parish council.[40] The Hooper family made a big contribution from the early 1900s.[41] John William Hooper and his son Ernest were among the unpaid helpers who built the first village hall in 1923. Mrs A.M. Hooper was churchwarden in the 1930s.[42] Ernest Hooper was chairman of the parish council from 1947 to 1976, chairman of the village hall for the same period and was also involved with the Horticultural Society.[43] Richard Hooper followed in his father's footsteps as chairman of the parish council from 1984 to 1988 and as chairman of the village hall in the important period that led up to the completion and early days of the Millennium Hall, resigning in 2000.[44] Hoopers Mead housing development was named after the family.

By 2001 changes nationwide meant that birth statistics no longer related to parish and county. Census figures for Cliddesden in 2001 showed that 426 residents had been born in England and a further 18 in the rest of the United Kingdom, 25 in other parts of Europe, five in Africa, eight in the Middle East or Asia, and three in the Americas or Caribbean.[45]

Social Life

Gentry Sport

In the 18th and 19th centuries, the earls of Portsmouth reserved sporting rights for themselves, or their nominees, across their lands in Cliddesden. Leases, such as one in 1771, excluded 'all fishing, fowling, hawking, and hunting, and Eyres of hawks and herons and all games of partridges, pheasants, hares, deer and conies which shall breed or be upon the premises during the tenancy',[46] and in 1866, at Hatch Warren Farm, a lease reserved 'all Game, Woodcocks, Snipes, Wildfowls, Rabbits, Fish and Foxes, with exclusive liberty for the lessor and others nominated by him to ride, walk, hunt, shoot, fish, course, sport and come thereon'.[47]

39   *White's Dir.*, 1878.
40   *Hants and Berks. Gaz.*, 14 Mar. 1898, 19 Mar. 1910.
41   HRO, 15M84/E6/4/67; 15M84/3/1/1/55; 15M84/3/1/12/7.
42   HRO, 21M65/91F/2–3.
43   HRO, 30A05/PX1; 30A05/PX2, 200.
44   *Cliddesden Village Newsletter*, Mar. 2000; HRO, 30A05/PX2.
45   *Census*, 2001.
46   HRO, 12M49/A15/8.
47   HRO, 15M84/E6/1/24.

Figure 20 *The conservatory/ballroom at Audleys Wood c.1930.*

Audleys Wood, 1880–1951

A gentry house, Audleys Wood, was built in the 1880s and was a private residence until 1951. The owners included Thomas Pain, a director of Tattersalls the bloodstock auctioneers, William Bradshaw and three generations of the Simonds family, founder and directors of a brewery company in Reading.[48] During the Second World War the house was occupied by William Berry, 1st viscount Camrose (d. 1954), owner and editor-in-chief of the *Daily Telegraph* (1937–54).[49] This was a sporting estate and included Pensdell Farm within its grounds. In addition, Louis de Luze Simonds (d. 1916) held sporting rights over Hatch Warren Farm, Manor Farm, Church Farm and Swallick Farm. Sale particulars of 1930 advertised: 'Good Hunting can be had in the neighbourhood (South Berks., Vine, Craven and Garth Hunts) and there are several Golf Courses within easy reach'. Audleys Wood itself had pleasure grounds and three grass tennis courts.[50]

A conservatory/ballroom was added to the house in *c.*1900. Large balls were held there, including an annual Servants' Ball. Food was provided by Buzzards in London's Oxford Street. Christmas parties were held for the villagers, with Mr and Mrs Bradshaw, and then the Simonds family, taking the place of the lord of the manor in many respects.[51]

Community Activities and Public Buildings

In the 19th century facilities for community life apart from the parish church became available. By 1850 beer was sold in the central one of the three cottages which with the

---

48   HRO, 5M62/22/844; *Hants and Berks. Gaz.*, 12 Oct. 1889; *Census*, 1901–11; HRO, 5M62/34/486.
49   www.friendsofwillis.hampshire.org.uk/story_of_hackwood.htm (accessed 12 Aug. 2014). Lord Camrose's home at Hackwood Park was occupied by a Canadian military hospital.
50   HRO, 68M72/DDZ17.
51   Cliddesden Women's Institute, *Centenary Scrapbook* (unpubl.,1965).

other two was to become the Jolly Farmer public house[52] and later in the century the opening of the Board school and Methodist chapel added venues and opportunities for social gatherings. In 1923 a village hall was built on land given by Beatrice, countess of Portsmouth, opposite the Old School House.[53] Volunteers transported two First World War huts from Bramley and erected them on their new site.[54] This served the village well for many years but was replaced by a larger, well-equipped Millennium Hall, opened in June 1999. A building grant of £139,250 was obtained from the Millennium Commission and the site – disused allotments at the top of Church Lane – was sold by the 10th earl of Portsmouth to the hall trustees for £1.[55]

Initiatives designed to provide adult education and to engage young men and boys in positive activities were established in the second half of the 19th century. A workmen's club and reading room had 38 members in 1851.[56] A Working Men's Institute consisting of a night school, with two teachers, and a reading room situated in the rectory, which offered daily newspapers amongst other material, had 29 members in 1888. William Bradshaw of Audleys Wood was president and the institute was run by a committee of seven parishioners.[57]

A branch of the Women's Institute was established in the village in 1922 and celebrated its 90th anniversary in 2012. In 2015 the Institute had 32 members, about one third from Cliddesden, others coming from Basingstoke and surrounding villages.[58] The Cliddesden, Farleigh Wallop and Ellisfield Horticultural Society first met in 1947, a time when many residents had enough land to allow self-sufficiency in vegetables and to keep the traditional pig. 'Catch the greased pig' was one of the features of the summer show.[59] The society held its four annual events in 2015: a spring show, a plant sale, a best garden competition and a summer show. Since 2004 a community conservation group has undertaken work to maintain and improve the natural habitats for wildlife, plants and trees. In 2012 members of the group were amongst other villagers who formed a limited company, Cleresdene Land Ltd., to purchase a field in Farleigh Road which they planted as a wild-flower meadow.[60]

Sport played its part in village life. A cricket team was formed in 1901, the original pitch lying on land opposite Southlea.[61] Since 1987 cricket was played at Farleigh Wallop in the grounds of Farleigh House. A football team was also formed in the early 20th century and played on the glebe land opposite the Three Horseshoes. It joined with Farleigh Wallop, the black and white colours being those of Farleigh. The club folded in

---

52   HRO, 10M57/SP70.
53   HRO, 30A05/PX5.
54   www.cliddesden.jalbum.net (accessed 1 Jul. 2015). *Cliddesden Village Hall Opening Ode* by Mrs Simonds commemorated the men involved.
55   HRO, 30A05/PX5.
56   *Rel. Census*, 185.
57   *Hants and Berks. Gaz.*, 11 Feb. 1888, 5.
58   *Hill and Dale*, Nov. 2012, 34.
59   *Design Statement*, 6.
60   Alison Mosson, pers. comm., 2015; www.companycheck.co.uk/company/0801134/cleresden-land-ltd (accessed 22 Aug. 2015).
61   *Hants and Berks. Gaz.*, 5 Jul. 1901.

Figure 21 *Cliddesden Millennium Village Hall, opened in 1999.*

the late 1950s but a new club was started in the early 1970s and was active in the 1977–8 season.[62]

In 2015, weekly activities in the Millennium Hall consisted of a parent and toddlers group, Brownies, a sports and social club and several dance classes. A monthly film evening, organised by the Social and Entertainment Club, coffee mornings, meetings of clubs and societies, occasional events, such as a Harvest Festival lunch and auction of produce, as well as many individual or family celebrations show that the hall was well used. Twice-yearly theatrical productions by the Cliddesden Players, a summer show and a Christmas pantomime, appeared to be settled parts of the social calendar.[63] *Hill and Dale*, a church magazine for the parishes of Ellisfield, Farleigh Wallop, Dummer and Cliddesden and the *Cliddesden Village Newsletter*, produced by the parish council, advertised events and provided useful community information. An online village archive collected by Paul Beevers was a valuable local-historical resource. [64]

Education

Educational Provision before 1870

A school for the poor children of Cliddesden and Farleigh Wallop was established at the very early date of 1656 in the centre of Cliddesden village. Ann Doddington, eldest daughter of Sir Henry Wallop (I) made a gift of £200 to her brother Robert Wallop towards the building and maintenance of this school.[65] Other gifts and endowments enabled the school to continue.[66] Nomination of the master was by the lord of the manor jointly with the minister and churchwardens. The number of pupils was said to be

62 Bob Kew, pers. comm., 2015; *Cliddesden Village Newsletter*, Jan. 1978.
63 www.cliddesden-hall.hampshire.org.uk (accessed 22 Sept. 2015).
64 www.cliddesden.jalbum.net (accessed 17 Jan. 2017).
65 HRO, 15M84/5/9/5/10; *Charities Report*, 400; Bingley, *Hampshire*.
66 Below, Cliddesden – Charities.

Figure 22 *Old School House in 2013. It was known as Charity Cottage in the 1930s.*

'indefinite, it being for the benefit of orphans and other poor children of Cliddesden-cum-Farley'.[67] By 1788 there were 30 pupils.[68] A record of 1801 describes the school: 'There is at Clydesden a free school endowed by Mrs Ann Doddington with £10 per annum, a good school house for the master and a field of pasture'.[69] By 1818, 60 children from the two parishes were in attendance and 36 children attended a Sunday school but it was struggling financially. It was reported that: 'The poor possess the means of education, but any addition made to the salary of the endowed school, would be most gratefully received'.[70]

A second school existed in 1833 attended by ten children, paid for by their parents. Girls outnumbered boys in both weekday and Sunday schools. Twenty-one boys and 31 girls attended the free school, five boys and five girls attended the private school and eight boys and 25 girls attended the Sunday school.[71] The free school was rebuilt in 1851 at the expense of the 3rd earl of Portsmouth [72] and had three schoolrooms and a house.[73] By 1851 there were 70 children attending both the weekday school and the Sunday school.[74] However, by 1867 numbers had dropped to nearly half that with only 13 boys and 26 girls in attendance although the population of Cliddesden and Farleigh Wallop had increased in the same period.[75] The reason for this marked decrease in pupils is unknown.

67 *Parson and Parish*, 40.
68 Ibid., 267.
69 HRO, 15M84/5/9/5/10; Bingley, *Hampshire*. The origin of the £10 endowment remained a source of debate for many years, see below, Cliddesden – Charities.
70 *Educ. of Poor Digest*, 823. Other parishes also sought financial help.
71 *Educ. Enquiry Abstract*, 841.
72 *White's Dir.*, 1859.
73 HRO, 21M65/B5/2.
74 Ibid.
75 *School Inquiry*, 386.

1870–1902

By 1871 the free school in Cliddesden had closed. Twenty-two children attended
a private school in the village – whether this was the school that existed in 1831 is
unclear. There was no school in Farleigh Wallop and only a small private school in
Ellisfield.[76] Following the Education Act of 1870, a school board for the United District
of Cliddesden was established in March 1873. It appears that the board was imposed
on Cliddesden and the neighbouring parishes of Farleigh Wallop and Ellisfield because
there was no provision for free education in these villages and insufficient progress made
in addressing this state of affairs.[77] The absence of a resident lord of the manor may have
been a contributing factor in this situation. Board schools were not always welcomed
partly because their funding was largely through the rates, an expense quickly criticised
by those who had to pay.[78]

The school opened in 1876, on land sold by the 5th earl of Portsmouth for £22
10s. 0d.[79] Isolated on a hilltop, it lay within Farleigh Wallop parish on the boundary
with Cliddesden and at a considerable distance from each of the three settlements.[80]
For Cliddesden children it meant a walk of nearly a mile up a steep hill in exposed
countryside. The building was of brick and flint under a slate roof and consisted of a
schoolroom, classroom and an adjoining three-bedroomed house for the master.[81] An
extension for two cloakrooms was built in 1898 and extra land was gifted by the 9th earl
in 1950.[82]

Edward Ballard was headmaster from 1878, retiring in 1922.[83] Pupil numbers varied,
reaching 106 in 1907, although attendance was not always good.[84] The school was
affected by epidemics of contagious illnesses such as scarlet fever, when the Medical
Officer closed the school for eight days in July 1898, and a serious outbreak of measles
in 1901 which led to closure for five weeks.[85] Absences to help with seasonal work in
the fields included the hay and corn harvests, potato-lifting and hop-picking.[86] Truancy
caused by boys beating for the shoots on the estate, earning a few pence, was common
here as elsewhere in the county.[87] The headmaster reported that the 'Michaelmas
changing took away a lot of bright children'[88] and severe weather also prevented
children's attendance.[89]

76   *Retn of Parishes*, 146.
77   *London Gaz.*, 22 Feb.1873; *School Boards*, 36.
78   *Hants Advertiser*, 15 Nov. 1879: Cliddesden U.D. was assessed to pay 7d. in the £ on the rateable value of
     the district for the year ended 29 Sept. 1878. Rates varied from 1¼d. (St Mary Extra) to 21d. (Wield).
79   HRO, 15M84/E6/4/234.
80   The history of Cliddesden School after 1876 is continued in this chapter despite its new site in Farleigh
     Wallop parish.
81   HRO, 15M84/E6/4/41.
82   HRO, 15M84/2/1/6/10.
83   HRO, 23A01/A5, 7. A break occurred during his appointment.
84   HRO, 23A01/A5, 24.
85   TNA, MH 12/10697; Clidd. log summary.
86   HRO, 23A01/A5, 57: for example, the school closed for four weeks in 1912 during the hay harvest.
87   Clidd. log summary; E. Hallett, *Ampfield Village School* (Chippenham, 1996), 33, 36.
88   HRO, 23A01/A5, 15. Annual hiring of farm workers took place on 29 Sept.
89   Clidd. log summary.

Figure 23 *Cliddesden School, showing the large windows of the original classrooms. A new addition to the school built in 2001 can be seen on the right.*

1902–1944

The standard of education received mixed reports from HMI and resources were clearly limited. In 1904 it was recognised that it 'was impossible for the master to do justice to children in six standards with only the help of a monitress'.[90] The inspector commented in 1911 that subjects such as geography and literature were not well taught due to lack of suitable books[91] and in 1922 that the 'teacher was doing his best under difficult circumstances'.[92] There were regular tests on religious knowledge from the diocesan inspector. The children did well in these. In addition to the usual curriculum, boys were taught gardening and husbandry, for example caring for pigs and poultry, and girls learned needlework which on completion was sold for the benefit of the school.[93] During the First World War the school contributed towards the war effort by selling waste paper and collecting horse chestnuts for cordite manufacture.[94] In October 1917 evacuees came from a bombed area of London and stayed for one week.[95]

90   HRO, 23A01/A5, 10.
91   TNA, ED 21/6386.
92   TNA, MH 12/10697.
93   Clidd. log summary.
94   HRO, 23A01/A5, 87, 92.
95   TNA, ED 21/6386; Clidd. log summary. J. Hare and others, *Mapledurwell* (2012), 61: children from Walworth and Bow were evacuated to Mapledurwell for short periods in Oct. and Nov. 1917.

Physical conditions were poor. Toilet provision consisted of peat turfs for boys and pails for girls. From 1903 concerns were raised about the condition of drinking water, declared unwholesome by the county surveyor.[96] A temporary measure was introduced in 1928 of water being delivered by a farm water-cart.[97] A supply was eventually laid on by Portsmouth Estates in *c.*1929.[98] Classrooms were heated by coal or coke stoves and the school relied on natural light provided through the large windows. Problems continued with the long walk to school; children sometimes arrived wet and muddy causing HMI to report on a lack of cleanliness of pupils and the master had to supply spare clothes when needed.[99] In 1924 the headmaster on his own initiative provided hot cocoa at midday for the pupils.[100]. A school bus service started for Ellisfield children in 1929 and was later extended to Cliddesden.[101] School dinners were introduced in 1936.[102]

In the 1930s girls over 11 years old started to receive domestic science lessons, at first in the village hall and then, during the 1950s, at The Shrubbery secondary school in Basingstoke.[103] Boys went to Basingstoke for woodwork classes.[104] From the 1930s some children gained scholarships to grammar schools in Basingstoke.[105] The School Foundation offered grants to such children as well as assisting with payments for music lessons and providing prizes.[106]

During the Second World War, 65 evacuees and their teachers were received from Regents Park Infants School, in Shirley, Southampton. Local and evacuee children were taught in two tranches of three days each, including Saturday. Gas mask drills were implemented and senior children were instructed in the use of stirrup pumps and sandbags.[107] In 1941 a plane crashed near the school, soldiers were billeted in the infants' classroom and the village halls of Cliddesden and Ellisfield were brought into use as alternative teaching areas.[108] By 1942, when a number of evacuees had returned home, classes were amalgamated and full-time schooling resumed. [109]

1945–2015

In the 1940s and 1950s children no longer stayed away from school to work in the fields apart from those who accompanied their families on the annual hop-picking camps in the district.[110] Facilities improved with the installation of Elsan toilets in 1955 and the water supply was adopted by the Mid-Wessex Water Board in the same year.[111] Tilley

96   HRO, 23A01/A5, 9.
97   Ibid., 127.
98   HRO, 15M84/E6/4/229.
99   TNA, ED 21/6386; Clidd. log summary.
100 HRO, 23A01/A5, 118; Clidd. log summary.
101 *Basingstoke Gaz.*, 20 Jan. 1978.
102 Clidd. log summary.
103 HRO, 23A01/A5, 132; Clidd. log summary.
104 HRO, 23A01/A5, 163.
105 HRO, 23A01/A2; Clidd. log summary.
106 Below, Cliddesden – Charities.
107 Clidd. log summary.
108 Ibid.
109 Ibid.
110 Ibid. Destinations included Newnham and Alton.
111 Clidd. log summary; HRO, 23A01/A5, 180.

lamps were provided in 1959 for the master and cooking/cleaning staff, Calor gas was installed in 1960, used for heating, lighting and cooking and flush WCs were fitted in 1965; electricity followed in 1973, a very late provision compared with other schools in Hampshire and due, no doubt, to the isolated site.[112] In 1964 the inspector commended the teachers on the standards they had achieved despite limited accommodation.[113] The curriculum became more varied with IT learning introduced in the 1980s when netball and football teams were also formed.[114] Gardening, established in the early days of the school, continued and was still on the timetable in 2015.

Numbers were at their lowest in 1960 with only 56 pupils on the roll, but rose to 84 by 1974.[115] The steady expansion of Basingstoke and the admission of children from surrounding housing areas brought significant change. By 1983, 33 per cent of the children were from Brighton Hill and the proportion of children from outside the original three parishes continued to rise as Kempshott, Hatch Warren and Beggarwood were developed. Added pressure on accommodation came in 1996 when the school was asked to increase numbers after Beech Down School in Brighton Hill burnt down.[116] An extension in 2001 resulted in an extra classroom; there was also a PE/assembly hall, kitchen, two study rooms, a library and a school office. The school also had two gardens and a small orchard in the playing field.[117]

In 2015, in addition to the head teacher, the school had a complement of seven teachers, supported by eight classroom assistants and administrative staff, with 111 pupils. Of these children, 18 came from Cliddesden, two from Farleigh Wallop, seven from Ellisfield, two from Dummer and 82 from Basingstoke.[118] It was one of the few rural primary schools around Basingstoke to remain open, and the influx of pupils from the town was a significant factor in enabling its survival. The school enjoyed an enthusiastic group of 'Friends' who raised money to support activities, whilst former pupils could be helped with their further and higher education by grants from the Cliddesden and Farleigh Wallop Educational Trust.

A day nursery operated in The Old Dairy from 1992 to 2013. Otters Nursery School opened in the same building in 2014, accommodating 42 children up to the age of five years.[119]

Charities and Welfare

Endowed Charities

A number of endowed charities in the parish benefitted the poor, the school or sometimes both. The long-serving rector Edward Mooring (d. 1673) left the considerable

---

112 HRO, 23A01/A5, 198, 208, 212, 277.
113 TNA, ED 161/6241; HRO, 23A01/A5, 230.
114 HRO, 23A01/A5, 182; Clidd. log summary.
115 Clidd. log summary.
116 HRO, 23A01/A5, 274, 285.
117 Information provided by the school, 2015.
118 Ibid.
119 www.findmyschool.co.uk/schooldetails (accessed 15 Apr. 2015); *Basingstoke Gaz.*, 20 Sept. 2013.

sum of £320, to be invested at £16 a year, for the poor of the parish [120] but also expressed a wish that the school established by Mrs Doddington be maintained and a master kept there.[121] Dorothy Wallop, née Bluett (d. 1704), bequeathed £10 for the poor of the parish of Cliddesden.[122] This appears not to have been paid out with her other legacies but an endowment, called the Dorothy Bluett (Wallop) bequest, produced £10 a year for the school.[123]

Theodosia Wallop (d. 1656) left £100 for placing poor children from the parishes of Farleigh and Cliddesden as apprentices.[124] At his death in 1731 the rector, William Dobson, held the £100 given by Theodosia Wallop, and willed that the principal and interest be paid as well as bequeathing a further £100 for the poor.[125] The Fellowes Charity established by the will of Thomas Fellow of Farleigh Wallop in 1738 left £30 to the poor, to be invested and the income distributed yearly by the rector.[126] An 1812 account shows 'for eight years, bread money at 19s. a year' and £28 8s. 0d. spent in apprenticing poor children from Cliddesden and Farleigh Wallop.[127] In addition to a gift for the poor, David Davies, rector (d. 1813), left £50 upon trust, the dividends 'to be applied half-yearly for the Endowed or Charity school in Cliddesden'.[128]

In 1895 confusion and concerns about the source, purpose and administration of the various charities led the parish council to call a public meeting and subsequently to ask the Charity Commission to formulate a scheme that would incorporate all the charities benefitting Cliddesden and Farleigh Wallop. The council named 'Fellowe's Gift, Mrs Dorothy Wallop's Bequest and Mrs Ann Doddington's Benefaction of School House at Cliddesden'.[129] After extensive enquiries, a Charity Commission scheme sealed on 25 April 1899 settled matters.[130] The Fellowes Charity and that of an unknown donor were merged as one charity, to be known as the Fellowes Charity, whilst a school charity was established consisting of the 'Schoolhouse and Endowment'. The income of each of the two charities was to be divided into four equal parts to be applied in a ratio of three parts to Cliddesden and one part to Farleigh Wallop.

In 1899 the newly formed Fellowes Charity was worth £164 14s. 8d., giving a yearly sum of £4 10s. 4d. to be distributed by the trustees to the poor for such necessities as coal or clothing. Under the new scheme the stock, invested in Consols, was transferred into the name of the Official Trustee of Charitable Funds.[131] In 1903, a typical year in the early 20th century, £3 was given to a clothing club in Cliddesden, £1 to a similar club

120 TNA, PROB 11/343/217.
121 HRO, 15M84/5/9/5/10.
122 HRO, 44M69/F3/6.
123 Ibid.; HRO, 15M84/E6/4/234.
124 TNA, PROB 11/258/289.
125 TNA, PROB 11/646/467; *Parson and Parish*, 40.
126 HRO, 1738B/21. Thomas Fellow appears to have had no connection with the Fellowes branch of the Wallop family. The misspelling of his name led to the charity being called 'Fellowes'.
127 *Charities Report*, 399–400.
128 TNA, PROB 11/1940/346.The trustees were Henry Fellowes, the Hon. Newton Fellowes and Henry Newton Fellowes.
129 HRO, 15M84/E6/4/234.
130 HRO, 15M84/5/9/5/10 – about 40 letters and memoranda formed part of the investigation; HRO, 15M84/E6/4/234.
131 HRO, 35M84/148.

in Farleigh Wallop and 10s. was distributed to individuals.[132] In the 1940s Miss Badger, the rector's sister, distributed £4 annually.[133] By 2001 the funds were exhausted and the charity was removed from the charity commissioners' register.[134]

Two sources of income supported the School Charity: letting the former school house and the 'endowment' (not named). Known as Charity Cottage in the 1930s, rent for the old school house and adjoining blacksmith's shop rose with time from £12 a year, in 1899, until its eventual sale in 1997.[135] The proceeds of the sale greatly increased the charity's funds. It appears that the charity commissioners considered the Dorothy Bluett endowment and the remnant of the Ann Doddington endowment to be one and the same amount and that only one £10 annual payment be due from the Portsmouth estates, made in the form of a rent-charge.[136] During the period 1937 to 1953 this was sent to the Dorothy Bluett Charity by the estate and forwarded to the school board by the Dorothy Bluett trustees.[137] It is not known when payments ceased.

The School Charity was specified for use in binding apprentices, prizes, payments to encourage continuance at school and exhibitions for higher education.[138] The name was changed to The School Foundation in 1904[139] and was further changed in 2000 to The Cliddesden and Farleigh Wallop Educational Trust. The trust assists young people under the age of 25 years to further their academic, musical and physical education. £17,287 was spent in the year ending 31 December 2015.[140] The Friends of Cliddesden School was established in 1990 for the support of the education of the pupils of Cliddesden School; £3,872 was spent in the year ending 31 July 2015.[141]

Poor Relief

In the 16th century charitable gifts to the poor were made by both clergy and laity. The rector, Thomas Lodge (d. 1552), left 3s. 4d. to the poor men's box and 12d. to all the single young men and women of Cliddesden to be given them at the time of their marriage 'so that they continue in the said parish'.[142] Thomas Walker (d. 1549) of Penns left 26s. 8d. to the poor [143] and Amy Wodeson, a widow (d. 1559), left a bushel of wheat for the poor.[144] In 1587 Sir Henry Wallop (I) gave 2s. a quarter for a year to a blind man dwelling in Cliddesden and 5s. to the poor people of Cliddesden.[145] Similar gifts in the 17th century ranged from 3s. 4d. to £2.[146]

132 Ibid.
133 HRO, 15M84/E6/4/234.
134 www.charity-commission.gov.uk: removed charity no. 210099, 5 Apr. 2001 (accessed 20 Aug. 2014).
135 www.gov.uk/search-property-information-land-registry: title no. HP529880 (accessed 23 Oct. 2014).
136 HRO, 15M84/E6/4/234.
137 Ibid.
138 Ibid.; www.charity-commission.gov.uk: Scheme 1297/99, 25 Apr. 1899 (accessed 20 Aug. 2014).
139 For that part of the charity to be applied to educational purposes see www.charity-commission.gov.uk:
      Scheme 3209/4, 18 Oct.1904 (accessed 20 Aug. 2014).
140 www.charity-commission.gov.uk: no. 307159 (accessed 3 Jun. 2016).
141 Ibid., no. 1041400 (accessed 3 Jun. 2016).
142 HRO, 1552B/057.
143 HRO, 1549B/62; Penns – one of the variant names for Pensdell Farm.
144 HRO, 1559U/225.
145 HRO, 44M69/E5/3.
146 TNA, PROB 11/96/39; 11/203/679; HRO, 1612B/029; 1613B/03; 1631B/12; 1649A/36.

Charitable help for the poor continued in the 18th and early 19th centuries. John Wallop, viscount Lymington left £20 for the poor of the parish of Cliddesden and a similar amount for the poor of Farleigh Wallop in 1749.[147] The 1st earl of Portsmouth left £100 to be distributed 'in charity' in the parishes which lay within his Hampshire manors.[148] Bequests from rectors of Cliddesden and Farleigh Wallop included Richard Exton (d. 1759) 10 guineas, Benjamin Woodroffe (d. 1770) £10, Christopher Fox (d. 1803) £20 and David Davies (d. 1813) £30.[149] These gifts were for the poor of both parishes.

Statutory support for the poor was provided out of the parish rate income which in 1750 amounted to £15 4s. 8d.[150] However, by 1776 overseers of the poor disbursed £92 2s.10d. in poor relief.[151] This sum rose to £251 4s. 0d. in 1803, soared to £621 5s. 0d. in 1818, the period after the end of the French wars, and peaked at around £636 between 1830 and 1832.[152] Cliddesden's population was 239 in 1801 and poor relief appears to have been above that of parishes of a similar size in the Basingstoke area. Only three complaints that relief had not been paid, or was insufficient, were made between 1779 and 1801.[153] In 1818, in both a benevolent act and an attempt to diminish the pressure on the poor rates, the farmers of the parish supplied every cottager with a portion of land for the cultivation of potatoes, the produce of which was calculated to be equal to the yearly consumption of each family; the rector, David Davies, provided the seed potatoes.[154] David Davies also made small loans available for cultivators to purchase seed and was reported as reducing the amount of tithes payable to him by up to 25%.[155]

The increasing sums spent on the poor in Cliddesden typify a national trend, a reason why a new system of poor relief was sought in an attempt to curtail expenditure. In 1834 the Poor Law Amendment Act introduced poor-law unions and Cliddesden became part of the Basingstoke Union. Vagrants or destitute parishioners might be admitted to the Union workhouse situated in Old Basing. Two pauper patients, classified as 'insane', were sent on removal orders to the county asylum, Knowle Hospital at Fareham, in 1859.[156] Between 1835 and 1845 out-relief included two midwifery payments, one infant's funeral costs and a number of loans were made ranging from 5s. to £1; no evidence exists of these loans being repaid.[157] Cottages in the fork of the road to Preston Candover and the road to Ellisfield belonged to the overseers of Cliddesden, and were presumably used as 'poor cottages'. They were still in the ownership of the overseers in 1855.[158] The parish contribution to the common fund of the Union was £522 in the financial year 1926/7.[159]

---

147 TNA, PROB 11/783/67.

148 TNA, PROB 11/882/235.

149 TNA, PROB 11/849/371; PROB 11/960/156; PROB 11/1396/110; PROB 11/1940/346.

150 HRO, 44M69/J3/1.

151 *Poor Abstract, 1777*, 453.

152 *Poor Abstract, 1804*, 450; *Poor Rate Rtns*, (1822), 154; (1835), 173.

153 HRO, 44M69/G3/871; 44M69/G3/734; 44M69/G3/541.

154 *Jackson's Oxford Jnl*, 1 May 1819. The scheme was devised by the bishop of Bath and Wells.

155 *Bury and Norwich Post*, 21 Apr. 1830; *Morning Chron.*, 10 Jan. 1828.

156 HRO, 48M94/B6/489; 48M94/B6/1097.

157 HRO, PL3/5/2–5.

158 HRO, 15M84/2/1/6/3.

159 HRO, 68M72/DU18.

Settlement and Bastardy

Residence and paternity issues concerned the parish officers. In the period 1689–1820 there were 10 removal orders out of the parish, six of these to Farleigh Wallop, and seven orders were made into Cliddesden.[160] One settlement examination took place in 1748.[161] This suggests relative stability of population but emphasises the close links with Farleigh Wallop. Three bastardy examinations were carried out in 1747, 1769 and 1780. [162] In 1785 a mother, sent by a pass from a parish in Middlesex, was reported to 'hath run away and left her [2] children which have become chargeable to Cliddesden'. A warrant was issued for her arrest.[163]

Medical and Welfare Services

Parishioners were dependent on doctors or surgeons in Basingstoke whose services, prior to 1948 and the establishment of the National Health Service, required payment. A branch of the Hampshire Friendly Society was established in Cliddesden in 1900, a mutual insurance society providing financial aid in times of illness.[164] Informal help also existed in the parish – certain women who acquired knowledge through experience and assisted with childbirth, during illness and with laying out the dead. In the 1930s Edith Hibberd and Amy Hayward performed this important role.[165] Other provision included the Basingstoke Cottage Hospital, which opened in 1879, and the County Hospital at Winchester, both institutions reliant on voluntary donations. Richard Exton, rector, left £20 to the County Hospital in 1759, the year it moved within Winchester to its site in Romsey Road.[166] Thomas Pain of Audleys Wood gave £100 to the Cottage Hospital in 1881 and continued as a benefactor until his death in 1885.[167]

In 1951 Audleys Wood became a 50-bed home for the elderly, run by Hampshire County Council until 1986. From 1970 until 1996 Farleigh Dene was used as a children's home for 12 children of school age, also a county council provision. In both instances the majority of residents came from Basingstoke or elsewhere in north Hampshire.[168] A workshop for people with physical disabilities opened in the grounds of Audleys Wood in the late 1960s.[169] In 2016, with newly-built facilities, it operated as a day resource centre for people with disabilities.

160 HRO, 44M69/G3/241; 3M70/55/18; 3M70/55/2; 65M72/PO4/14; 44M69/G3/454; 44M69/G3/440; 3M70/56/50–51; 86M82/PO3/7; 44M69/G3/254.
161 HRO, 3M70/53/12.
162 HRO, 3M70/53/11; 44M69/G3/385; 44M69/G3/571.
163 HRO, 44M69/G3/643.
164 *Hants Advertiser*, 5 May 1900, 3.
165 BTH, Irene Holloway (BAHS 124).
166 TNA, PROB 11/849/394.
167 HRO, 8M62/6.
168 HRO, 57M71; H/ES2/3/3/14, 29; H/SS1/2–3.
169 HRO, H/ES2/3/3/29.

Manorial and Hundred Courts

IN THE 13TH CENTURY, THE LORDS of Cliddesden made occasional use of Basingstoke borough court to register deeds.[1] There are no manorial court records for Cliddesden or Farleigh Wallop, but there are two references in Sir Henry Wallop's bailiffs' accounts to Cliddesden payments at a manorial court, one a heriot in 1579–80, the other unspecified in 1582–3. By this date, the court may have consisted of a simple interview with a bailiff at Farleigh House.[2] The bailiffs' accounts also have occasional references to copyholds in Cliddesden, which would normally have been transferred from one tenant to the next in a manorial court, the court baron, but may likewise have happened more informally as occasion arose. As late as 1779 a new tenant was said to be a customary tenant owing suit to the court of Cliddesden with Farleigh.[3] At the next level of local government, the tenants of the tithings of Cliddesden and Hatch owed suit to the hundred court of Basingstoke. The bailiffs of the borough were overlords of the manors, and exercised the responsibility of the court leet through the hundred court: petty disputes and misdemeanours were settled at views of frankpledge there.[4] Payments for the national tax called 'fifteenths' were made on their behalf in 1587–8 by the bailiff of Farleigh Wallop out of Sir Henry's own funds.[5]

Parish Government and Officers

Cliddesden and Farleigh Wallop were united as an ecclesiastical benefice in 1579 but, whilst the parish registers were then combined, each retained its own parish officials.[6] Churchwardens and overseers of the poor were drawn from the ranks of the leading tenants, elected annually at a vestry meeting of ratepayers. Churchwardens had a range of ecclesiastical and secular functions and, although none of their account books survive, presentments made in 1692 by Richard Hockly and in 1697 by Henry Fry to the archdeacon concerning alleged adultery and non-attendance at church reveal some

1   Baigent and Millard, *Basingstoke*, 602, 606.
2   HRO, 44M69/E5/1.
3   HRO, 12M49/A15/9.
4   HRO, 148M71/2/1.
5   HRO, 44M69/E5/2.
6   Registers for Cliddesden cum Farleigh were combined from 1579 to 1837. Whether each parish had two churchwardens and two overseers of the poor or whether the posts were split between them is not clear. Cliddesden had only one overseer in 1773: HRO, 44M69/G3/454.

of their duties.[7] Sums spent by the overseers in support of the poor are known from parliamentary returns but their account books are lost, so exactly how the parish rate was spent is not clear.[8] William Spier, a farmer, was the first guardian elected as Cliddesden's board member on the Basingstoke Union, established as a result of the 1834 Poor Law Amendment Act and which assumed responsibility for poor relief.[9]

Cliddesden civil parish was established under the Local Government Act of 1894. It followed the boundaries of the ecclesiastical parish and until 1974 was within the rural district of Basingstoke. The occupations of the five members elected to the parish council – a farmer, shepherd, hosier, carpenter and woodman – show that the body charged with the conduct of local affairs had a representative spread of parishioners.[10] In 1896, the rector, Revd John Seymour Allen, and John Bird, newspaper proprietor, were among those elected.[11] John Bird became chairman and continued in office until his death in 1905, actively pursuing issues such as the administration of local charities.[12] The rector remained a member until 1934, serving for a remarkable period of 39 years and representing the parish on the rural district council for much of this period.[13] He was succeeded by Revd Arthur Badger who was a member of the parish council during the period of his incumbency (1935–60), served on the rural district council, taking a special interest in housing and sanitation, and was a poor law guardian.[14]

Ernest Hooper, who farmed Church and Manor Farms, was chairman of the parish council from 1947 to 1976.[15] Then, as in the 21st century, the council showed a determination to conserve the rural nature of the community in the face of Basingstoke's growth. Issues of continuing concern included the volume of traffic through the village on narrow, unsuitable roads, the state of the village pond, consideration of planning applications and the creation and support of facilities for the parish, such as the village hall.[16]

In 1974, under local government reorganisation, Cliddesden became a constituent parish of Basingstoke and Deane Borough Council.[17]

7   HRO, 202M85/3/264.
8   Above, Cliddesden – Social History.
9   HRO, PL3/5/1.
10   *Hants Chron.*, 6 Dec. 1894, 3.
11   *Hants and Berks. Gaz.*, 14 Mar. 1896, 8.
12   Above, Cliddesden – Social History.
13   *Hants and Berks Gaz.*, 19 Aug. 1949, 5.
14   HRO, 30A05/PX1.
15   Above, Cliddesden – Social History.
16   HRO, 30A05/PX1–7.
17   www.basingstoke.gov.uk (accessed 26 Apr. 2015).

THE RELIGIOUS HISTORY OF CLIDDESDEN has been closely linked with that of Farleigh Wallop and followed a very similar course. Nonconformity was virtually non-existent until the late 19th century when Wesleyan Methodists first met in the village. In the 20th and 21st centuries, the proximity of Basingstoke has offered parishioners choice in opportunities for worship.

Parochial Organisation

A church at Cliddesden is recorded in Domesday Book,[1] whilst the present parish church of St Leonard dates from the first half of the 12th century the dedication is not recorded before the 19th century.[2] It was known to have had its own rector by the early 14th century.[3] The neighbouring parish of Hatch also had a church in 1086[4] but in 1378 the bishop petitioned Richard II that it be discharged from paying tenths on the grounds of poverty and depopulation; two years later this request was granted as the church was in ruins and its value so small that no one would serve the cure and after this Hatch became merged in the parish of Cliddesden.[5]

In 1579 Farleigh Wallop was joined with Cliddesden,[6] thus uniting the religious life of the parishes for nearly four centuries until 1954 when this arrangement was dissolved.[7] Rectors were inducted to both Cliddesden and Farleigh Wallop. The rectory was that of Cliddesden and the church at Farleigh Wallop was sometimes referred to as a chapel of Cliddesden during this period.[8] In 1954 the long union of Cliddesden with Farleigh Wallop was dissolved and from 1954 to 1977 Cliddesden was joined with Winslade.[9] Cliddesden then became a benefice comprising only the parish of Cliddesden.[10] In 1983, a benefice was formed consisting of Cliddesden, Farleigh Wallop, Ellisfield and Dummer, sharing one priest and with a rectory at Ellisfield.[11] This became a single parish in 2008, known as Farleigh,[12] and in 2010 formed part of a new, united benefice of Farleigh,

1   *Domesday*, 115.
2   Pevsner, *North Hampshire*, 226.
3   *Reg. Woodlock*, 330.
4   *Domesday*, 121.
5   *Reg. Wykeham* II, 292, 321; *VCH Hants* IV, 147.
6   *Parson and Parish*, 39.
7   HRO, 67M72/PR5, copy of Order in Council pasted into register.
8   *Doing the Duty*, 30.
9   HRO, 67M72/PR5, copy of Order in Council pasted into register.
10   HRO, 2M81/PB18.
11   HRO, 21M65/Orders in Council/Cliddesden.
12   www.allsaintschurchdummer.hampshire.org.uk: parish of Farleigh (accessed 1 Oct. 2013).

Figure 24 *The church of St Leonard. The chancel added in 1888–9 can be seen with a change in colour of the roof tiles.*

Candover and Wield with a rector and an associate rector, the latter holding primary pastoral responsibility for the northern parishes including Cliddesden.[13]

Advowson

The advowson of both Cliddesden and Hatch has throughout followed the descent of the manor.[14] John de Valognes (I) lord of the manor, first presented a rector to Cliddesden in 1315,[15] John de Valognes (II) presented in 1333[16] and John de Valognes (III) presented rectors to Cliddesden several times between 1348–73[17] as well as to Hatch in 1349 and 1351.[18] In 1360, presentation to Hatch was made by the bishop, 'collation by devolution'; the reason for this intervention is not known.[19] Sir Nicholas de Valognes presented to Cliddesden in 1396.[20] From the middle of the 15th century the Wallop family held the manor and the advowson. The Crown – Elizabeth I – presented in 1577 after a long

13 Winchester Diocesan Office: pastoral scheme, Jul. 2010.
14 Above, Cliddesden – Landownership.
15 *Reg. Woodlock* II, 744.
16 *Reg. Stratford* I, 431.
17 *Reg. Edington* I, 48, 68, 102, 127; *Reg. Wykeham* I, 48.
18 *Reg. Edington* I, 105, 121.
19 *Reg. Edington* I, 181.
20 *Reg. Wykeham* I, 201.

vacancy [21] and another exception was made in 1673 when the Wallop patron was a minor.[22] Barton Wallop, rector from 1770–80, was not presented by his family but by James Hayes of Holyport, Berkshire, 'patron for the turn'.[23] In 1887 Isaac Newton Wallop, 5th earl of Portsmouth safeguarded the family interests by entering into a bond of £6,000 with Harry Sneyd Mather when presenting him to the rectory on condition that he would vacate it should he, the earl, wish one of his own sons to have the living.[24] The Winchester bishopric presented in 1961 during the time that Cliddesden was joined to Winslade.[25] The advowson for the benefice of Cliddesden, Farleigh Wallop, Ellisfield and Dummer, created in 1983, was held jointly by the earl of Portsmouth and the Diocesan Board of Patronage.[26] Presentation arrangements established for the new benefice in 2010 gave alternate patronage of either the Lord Chancellor or the bishop of Winchester, the appropriate diocesan body, the earl of Portsmouth and Sir John Baring, acting together.[27]

Glebe, Tithes and Rectory House

The living was valued at a modest £5 6s. 8d. in 1291.[28] The early years of the 14th century saw changed agricultural conditions and in 1341 the church endowment of one messuage, a garden, 16 a. of land and pasture was said to be worth only 32s. 10d. annually. The tithe of calves and other small tithes with offerings and mortuary payments amounted to 42.s 10d. in 1341, a reduced income for the rector from all sources.[29] By 1535 the value of the living had risen to £10 10s. 1d.[30] In 1728 a terrier of glebe land belonging to the parsonage of Cliddesden listed a rickyard and two gardens adjoining the parsonage house and one yard or backside, a meadow called Hackers of ¾ a. and 10½ a. of land called Bouling ally piece.[31] In 1841, the glebe comprised the same two small meadows, an arable field and the gardens surrounding the rectory house.[32] The tithe award of 1842 commuted the payment of tithes, all of which were owned by the rector, to £550 a year; the tithable acreage was 1,809 a., the whole parish apart from roads, buildings, glebe and waste land. A rent charge for glebe land of 10½ a. was fixed at £3.[33] Joined with Farleigh Wallop this made the living a wealthy one, well-illustrated by the substantial rectory house. In 1878 the combined living was valued at about £900 gross,[34]

21   Reg. Horne, f. 115.
22   Reg. Morley, f. 49. Anthony, count of Shaftesbury, chancellor of England, and Henry Vernon, baronet, presented.
23   HRO, 21M65/A2/2, f. 78.
24   HRO, 35M48/6/2020.
25   HRO, 35M48/6A/213.
26   HRO, 21M65/Orders in Council/Cliddesden.
27   Winchester Diocesan Office: pastoral scheme, Jul. 2010.
28   *Tax. Eccl.*, 212. By contrast, Steventon church was assessed at £10: ibid.
29   *Nonarum Inquisitiones*, 122.
30   *Valor Eccl.* II, 14.
31   HRO, 35M48/16/81.
32   TNA, IR 18/8949; HRO, 21M65/F7/53/1.
33   HRO, 21M65/F7/53/1.
34   *White's Dir.*, 1878.

whilst actual (net) clerical income was £435 9s. 5d. in 1899 and £516 12s. 6d. in 1915.[35] The church at Hatch was valued at £4 6s. 8d. in 1291[36] but by the time it was joined to Cliddesden it was in ruins.

The rectory occupied a prominent site in the village street, south of the pond and about ¼ mile from the church which lies to the east of the pond up a small curving lane. An 1841 catalogue of the effects of the late rector, David Davies, lists entrance hall and staircase, study, drawing room, five bedrooms, dressing room and store room, dining room, butler's pantry and closet, pantry, store room, kitchen, brew house and cellar.[37] An 1887 claim for dilapidations lists many more rooms including a servants' wing, housekeeper's room, and a coach house.[38] In 1843 the house was restored at a cost of £1,100.[39] By 1959 the rectory was found to be in urgent need of modernisation and far larger than needed.[40] In 1963 the Church Commissioners approved the sale of the rectory with 3 a. of land and an estimate of £7,829 was accepted for building a new parsonage house on glebe land in Woods Lane for which the Commissioners granted a 25-year mortgage of £5,650 in 1965.[41] This served as the rectory until 1982 when it was sold, the rectory at Ellisfield having been chosen as the rectory for the new benefice.[42]

Pastoral Care and Religious Life

The Middle Ages

The first known rector, Henry Trocard, is recorded as having served Cliddesden before 1308.[43] In that year Miles of Upton, although only an acolyte, was admitted as rector.[44] In 1315 he was granted a year's study leave,[45] followed by two years' study leave,[46] during which time Robert of Bereford was appointed 'in commendam', that is for a temporary period.[47] A number of rectors served the parish in the years 1348–9. Following the resignation of John Palfreour in 1348,[48] the brief incumbencies of John le Marshal,[49]

35   HRO, 21M65/B4/5–6.
36   *Tax. Eccl.*, 212.
37   HRO, 10M57/SP354.
38   HRO, 21M65/H2/1/123.
39   *White's Dir.*, 1878.
40   HRO, 56M82/B76/3.
41   HRO, 56M82/A2/2, 43; 21M65/DD91.
42   HRO, 55M82/B4/29.
43   *Reg. Woodlock* I, 330. For the original spelling of Trocard see HRO, 21M65/A1/2, f. 100.
44   *Reg. Woodlock* I, 324.
45   Ibid., 629.
46   *Regs. Sandale and Asser*, 28.
47   *Reg. Woodlock* II, 744.
48   *Reg. Edington* I, 48.
49   Ibid; otherwise known as John de Frollebury, *Reg. Edington* I, 46.

Gilbert atte Mulle,[50] William Elyot,[51] and Thomas le Halterwrighte,[52] reflect the ravages caused by the Black Death. Priests administering the last rites suffered a high death rate; Winchester diocese had the highest number of clergy deaths in the country during this period.[53] Movement took place between Cliddesden and Farleigh churches: William Elyot moved from Cliddesden to Farleigh in 1348[54] and Thomas le Halterwrighte made a similar move in 1350.[55]

The church at Hatch struggled throughout the 14th century. Whilst it was said to have been 'expensively built',[56] its financial position deteriorated; clerical taxation in 1291 showed it to have a lower value than that of Cliddesden.[57] In 1306, the 'parson' of Hatch owed dues of 14s. 8d. to the archdeaconry of Winchester and these had risen to £1 6s. 0d. by July of that year. Attempts to seize goods in lieu of payments by the archdeacon's servants were rebuffed and the rector was excommunicated. This action appears to have had results as in April 1307 the dues in question were handed over to the Abbot and convent of Hyde, as directed.[58] Rectors at Hatch included John, called 'Uphulle', admitted in 1326, Robert de Whelere admitted in 1349 and Stephen Wyot who succeeded him in 1351.[59] Wyot's rapid preferment from subdeacon in March of that year, when he was admitted as rector, to deacon on 2 April and priest on 16 April probably indicate the shortages of clergy caused by the Black Death and the measures taken to maintain a clerical presence in parishes.[60] The last rector of Hatch was William de Peynton who served from 1360.[61] The benefice was vacant by 1380 when, with few people and no resources, it was merged with Cliddesden.

For two centuries the religious life of Cliddesden appears to have been stable and the parishioners were served by a succession of clergy, some of whom spent lengthy periods of time as incumbents. Gilbert Jely was rector from 1462 to 1481[62] and John Whyte served from 1489 until, possibly, 1517.[63] The 1552 will and inventory of Thomas Lodge, 'parson of Clyddesdean',[64] give a sympathetic glimpse of a man who, with his three horses, six cows, a bullock and three score of ewes, farmed the glebe and cared for the poor people of the parish. He left to all single men aged 20 or upwards and all single women aged 18 or upwards in the parish the sum of 12d. to be paid on their marriage, 'so that they continue in the sayd paryshe'; he left 4d. to all the 'younglings of both kyndes', he forgave the debts of those who had borrowed money from him and he made generous gifts to the poor of Cliddesden, Basingstoke, Worting, Dummer, Ellisfield, Winslade and

50   *Reg. Edington* I, 55.
51   Ibid., 68.
52   Ibid., 102.
53   P. Ziegler, *The Black Death* (1969), 145.
54   *Reg. Edington* I, 100.
55   Ibid., 119.
56   *Reg. Wykeham* II, 292.
57   *Tax. Eccl.*, 212.
58   *Reg. Woodlock* II, 910, 920, 921.
59   *Reg. Stratford* I, 313; *Reg. Edington* I, 105, 121.
60   *Reg. Edington* II, 824, 827, 829.
61   *Reg. Edington* I, 181.
62   Reg. Waynflete I, f. 113v; Reg. Waynflete II, f. 85.
63   Reg. Courtney, f. 39; HRO, 21M65/B1/1.
64   HRO, 1552B/057.

his native Stour Provost, in Dorset. Whether Lodge forgave Dame Rose Wallop the £22 she disputed his having lent her and her husband, Sir Robert Wallop, is not known.[65]

The will of Francis Prince, a wealthy yeoman (d. 1557) demonstrates the restoration of Catholicism in the reign of Queen Mary. He asked that his body be buried in the churchyard of Cliddesden and left 6s. 8d. so that he could be prayed for in perpetuity. His bequests included 4d. to the mother church in Winchester and a ewe sheep to each of the churches of 'Fareley, Illesfeld and Winslade'.[66] Parishioners and clergy were slow to adapt to the 1559 Elizabethan settlement of religion. A 1560 will opened with a traditional Catholic invocation to 'our Lady St Mary'.[67] John Cooke, rector from 1552, was deprived in 1562,[68] presumably his papal sympathies making him unwilling to accept the 1559 settlement.

The Reformation – 1800

Baptism, marriage and burial registers of Cliddesden date from 1636 and include those of Farleigh Wallop until 1839. There are gaps in the burial register between 1643 and 1656, in the marriage register between 1643 and 1660 and in the baptism register from 1654–9,[69] the Civil War and Interregnum causing, as elsewhere, disruption in record keeping. The parish was not immune from the religious and political upheavals of the 17th century. Oliver Awbrey, rector from 1599 was deprived in 1636.[70] Edward Mooring, who succeeded him, was ejected in 1655 and replaced during the Interregnum by a puritan, Martin Morland.[71] Morland, a resident in the parish, baptised his own sons, Benjamin and Martin, in 1658 and 1660.[72] Mooring was reinstated in 1660 at the Restoration and continued to serve as rector until his death in 1673.[73]

A number of notable clergy served the parish in the late 17th and 18th centuries. William Dobson, rector for 50 years from 1678 to 1731, was president of Trinity College, Oxford, dividing his time between Cliddesden and Oxford, serving both with diligence and leaving legacies for the poor in Cliddesden and in the parish of Garsington, Oxford.[74] Benjamin Woodroffe, a prebendary of Winchester cathedral and whose armorial ledger stone lies in the cathedral, may best be remembered for his strongly held views against popery. Rector from 1760, his will expresses his belief in salvation through faith in the most extravagant and hyperbolic language.[75] Woodroffe's successor in 1770, Barton Wallop, had a dubious notoriety. An example of pluralism, not uncommon in the 18th century, Barton Wallop held a series of Hampshire livings and the mastership of

65   Watney, *Wallop Family* I, xxvii.
66   HRO, 1557U/242.
67   HRO, 1560A/08/1.
68   H. Gee, *The Elizabethan Clergy and the Settlement of Religion, 1558–1564* (Oxford, 1898), 285. Cooke later became rector of Dogmersfield (Hants) where he died in 1595.
69   HRO, 31M82/PR1.
70   Reg. Bilson, f. 8.
71   A.G. Matthews (ed.), *Calamy Revised: Being a Revision of Edward Calamy's Account of the Ejected Ministers … 1660–2* (Oxford, 1934), 335.
72   HRO, 31M82/PR1.
73   Ibid.
74   TNA, PROB 11/646/467.
75   TNA, PROB 11/960/156.

Magdalene College, Cambridge, all in his family's gift. His appointment at Cambridge caused consternation, not only on the academic front but also with regard to his 'rackety life style'.[76]

A list of the goods belonging to the parish church of Cliddesden was made by Henry Hockley in 1728:

A Bible, Common Prayer Book, & A Book of Homilies.

A Pulpit cloath and cushion.

A Carpet for the Communion Table.

A Table cloath and napkin both Damask.

The plate wch belongs to Cliddesden and Farly is

A silver flaggon. A silver salver. A silver chalice, A silver chalice gilt. A silver plate.[77]

Episcopal visitations elicited further information about the size and activities of the parish. In 1725 a return was made indicating that: 'The parish of Cliddesden-cum-Farly is in compass about 9 or 10 miles ... 170 souls ... about 2 marriages, 4 births and 4 burials a year'. By 1788, when Christopher Fox was rector, the population had nearly doubled, standing at 310, with not more than two marriages, 12 births and five burials a year. There were no chapels, lecturer or Dissenters.[78]

1800–2014

Another rector holding multiple livings, John Garnett, the son of John, Church of Ireland bishop of Clogher, was rector from 1803 to 1813, resided at Over Wallop, near Andover, and was said to 'occasionally visit Clisden and Fairly'[79] In addition to a number of parochial preferments, Garnett became a prebendary of Exeter and dean of Exeter in 1810.[80] The duties of the parish were carried out by a curate, William Hasker, who lived with his father some three miles away at Chineham. Distance was apparently no problem; Hasker reported that he undertook his duties 'as punctually as if on the spot' and was paid £60 a year.[81]

In an 1828 register of benefices, Cliddesden was said to have 350 'souls'; 25 people had been confirmed in 1832 and 24 in 1835, with averages of 15.6 baptisms, 7.8 burials and 2.9 marriages a year in the ten years from 1821.[82] It was also noted that the rector should repair the chancel, that the clerk's wages were £1 4s. 0d. and that the curate's stipend was £100. The religious census, undertaken in 1851, records that Cliddesden, with a population of 314, had average church attendances of 90 for morning services and 100 for services held in the afternoon.[83] Some 50 years later, 51 communicants were entered on the church roll; three services were held in the parish church each Sunday as

76   P. Cunich and others, *A History of Magdalene College, 1428–1994* (Cambridge, 1994), 182.

77   HRO, 35M48/16/83.

78   *Parson and Parish*, 39, 267.

79   HRO, 21M65/E7/1/42; *Doing the Duty*, 30.

80   *Alumni Cantab.*, pt. 2, iii, 16; 21M65/B5/1; *ODNB*, s.v. Garnett, John (1707/8–1782), Church of Ireland bishop of Clogher (accessed 1 Jun. 2013).

81   HRO, 21M65/E7/1/42; *Doing the Duty*, 30.

82   HRO, 21M65/B5/2.

83   *Rel. Census*, 185.

well as three on Christmas Day, three on Good Friday, one on Ascension Day and one on saints' days. Average congregations were 35 on Sunday mornings, and 45 on Sunday evenings. The Sunday school had 88 children on the books with an average attendance of 59. Lay helpers included two voluntary visitors, two Sunday school teachers, a choir of ten male and two female members and two bell ringers. There was also a paid organist.[84]

The reaction to the foundation of a Wesleyan Methodist chapel in Cliddesden in 1880 may well have been influenced by the support shown by the 5th earl of Portsmouth who contributed financially to the costs of the first building and by Newton Wallop, the 6th earl, who spoke publicly on the importance of Nonconformity as a political as well as a religious force.[85] The clergy appear to have followed this lead and only occasional rivalries are known of between the respective congregations.[86]

Rectors from 1813 resided in the parish. The large rectory was a gentry house.[87] The 1841 sale catalogue of the late rector, David Davies, headed 'Genteel furniture, old wines and 400 ounces of Plate'[88] is indicative of his social status, whilst the contents of the library reveal his intellectual and religious interests.[89] Another wealthy rector, Joshua Willoughby Bryan, served the parish for 46 years from 1841 to 1887. In 1861 he had eight children aged 2–16 years living at home, a butler, groom, cook, two nurses, a housemaid and a kitchen maid.[90] By 1871 he also employed a footman.[91]

A grandson of the 4th earl of Portsmouth, John Seymour Allen, rector from 1894 to 1934, was also socially removed from his parishioners. In 1899 he reported that the moral condition of the parish was 'very low, but not worse than other rural parishes in the neighbourhood' and that Sunday was observed 'with great laxity'. He complained that,

> In as much as there is no resident squire or landlord, the church work suffers for want of some layman of position to set an example of moral conduct, and interest in Church matters to the farmers and agricultural labourers.[92]

In the first half of the 20th century gradual changes took place in the church. By 1932 a parochial church council of six members had been established and there was an electoral roll of 54.[93] With Arthur Badger's appointment as rector in 1934 change continued. [94] In 1936 he identified social conditions as 'poor, entirely agricultural save for Farleigh House and Audleys Wood', although he described housing as 'very good on the whole'. Intemperance was said to be 'almost nil' and sexual immorality was 'average for a country village'. The parochial church council had expanded to 17 members at this time,

---

84 HRO, 21M65/F7/53/1.
85 *Hants and Berks. Gaz.*, 7 Mar. 1903, 8: a speech at London Street Congregational church, Basingstoke, referring to the 1902 Education Act, unpopular amongst Nonconformists.
86 Below, Nonconformity.
87 Above, Glebe, Tithes and Rectory House.
88 HRO, 10M57/SP354.
89 HRO, 10M57/C89.
90 *Census*, 1861.
91 *Census,* 1871.
92 HRO, 21M65/B4/5.
93 HRO, 35M48/15/567.
94 HRO, 21M65/A2/13, f. 22.

whilst the average attendance at Sunday school had risen to 60.[95] The start of the Second World War brought fresh challenges. Two families shared the rectory with the rector and his sisters during the war. Memories of the cold and of the large, bare rooms contrast vividly with earlier times.[96]

Amalgamations and alterations in the pastoral arrangements of the Anglican church which took place in the second half of the 20th century were not always welcomed by parishioners; Cliddesden, as other parishes elsewhere, mourned the loss of a resident rector and its independence as a parish.[97] Services at St Leonard's were maintained and, from 1983, efforts were made by the four churches in the new benefice to work together with a common purpose in carrying out their Christian mission. Religious life was described in 2010 thus:

> St Leonard's welcomes all types of services ranging from the traditional through to the more contemporary, attracting a wide cross-section of people. Congregations usually number 15 at our Saturday evening BCP [Book of Common Prayer] Holy Communion service to about 40 at our All Age Worship service (1st and 3rd Sundays).There are about 12 baptisms a year [in the benefice] and about the same number of funerals and weddings. Stepping Stones, the parish Sunday school, is one of the major factors in a significant increase in the number of families and young people attending our services.

Mention is also made of the choir and of some 'excellent organists'. Seeking a new priest, the requirement was for someone, 'irrespective of gender, who would lead the spiritual life of the parish through teaching, sermons, pastoral care and prayer'.[98]

Nonconformity

Cliddesden appears to have had no Dissent until the 19th century.[99] The first evidence of Nonconformity is a meeting house certificate issued in 1837 for the dwelling house or premises in Cliddesden of Charles Bulpitt, labourer, intended as a place of religion and worship by an assembly or congregation of Protestants.[100] Some 40 years later an appeal of 1870, entitled *A Methodist Wilderness*, claimed that 'Basingstoke and villages within two hours walk contain more than 17,000 people and not one Wesleyan Chapel'.[101] Basingstoke opened its first Wesleyan chapel in 1875 and from 1877 a group of Methodists met in Cliddesden. On Whit Monday, 17 May 1880, the foundation stone of the first Wesleyan chapel in the village was laid. After the stone-laying ceremony a public tea was held in Mr Cobden's barn followed by a public meeting, presided over by

95 HRO, 21M65/B4/10.
96 BTH, Betty Godden (BAHS 060) and David Dean-Saunders (BAHS 072).
97 HRO, 55M82/B4/29.
98 www.allsaintschurchdummer.hampshire.org.uk: parish of Farleigh (accessed 1 Oct. 2013).
99 *Compton Census*, 83; *Parson and Parish*, 39, 267.
100 HRO, 21M65/F2/5/227.
101 Attwood, *Struggle*.

Figure 25 *The former Wesleyan Methodist chapel, remodelled into a house.*

the Basingstoke Circuit minister, the Revd Arthur Cooke.[102] This small, single-storey building adjacent to Church Farm cost £364. The chapel flourished and within six years not only were the debts incurred by building cleared but a new project was undertaken to add a school room and extend the chapel.[103]

Numbers of worshippers continued to increase and in 1905–6 a much larger, redundant chapel building was moved from Basingstoke and re-erected at Southlea, Farleigh Road.[104] John Bird, founder of the *Hants and Berks. Gazette* and Cliddesden resident, played an important part in enabling this major undertaking.[105] The new chapel gave greatly increased capacity, was registered for marriages and provided a venue for social as well as religious activities in the village.[106] The building was described as 'large, very urban with an ironstone front in Middle-Pointed Gothic.'[107]

Two events each year had particular significance: the Whitsun anniversary with special services on the Sunday and a 'Meeting and Tea' on Whit Monday, and Harvest Festival with a 'Harvest Home Tea' at Viables Farm in Basingstoke parish and a sale of produce. Choir and band concerts were held, including a concert for the unemployed in 1922.[108] A former member of the Wesleyan Sunday school recalled the period of 1914–20: 'About 90 children and teachers were there every Sunday morning and we would go for long walks in the afternoon led by the superintendant.'[109] Relations between the Wesleyans and Anglicans were not always harmonious. In the 1920s the rector expected

102 *Hants and Berks. Gaz.*, 22 May 1880.
103 HRO, 57M77/NMS12.
104 Ibid.; *Basingstoke Gaz.*, 30 Mar. 1984.
105 Attwood, *Struggle*.
106 HRO, 57M77/NMS12. The chapel was registered for marriages from 1906 to 1980.
107 Pevsner, *North Hampshire*, 227.
108 HRO, 57M77/NMS12.
109 www.cliddesden.jalbum.net: John Willows, Memories 1977 (accessed 9 Nov. 2016).

Figure 26 *Villagers helping to build the Methodist chapel, Southlea houses are in the background.*

all children to acknowledge him – girls to curtsey and boys to raise their caps – a cause of some resentment amongst Methodists in this small, close-knit community.[110]

The period up until the Second World War saw the zenith of Methodism in Cliddesden, followed by a slow decline. From the 1960s a few stalwarts maintained chapel life, the foremost of whom was Alice Taplin of Elm Cottage, chapel steward.[111] In 1972 alterations to provide a youth centre with a small chapel at the entrance were undertaken but by 1979 chapel attendance had dwindled to nothing.[112] It was closed for services, although used by the Boys' Brigade until sold in 1981.[113] In 2016 it was a private house.

The Church of St Leonard

The church of St Leonard is a small, single-celled building of flint and stone with buttresses at the corners, and intermediately, with a tiled roof. It comprises a nave and chancel, organ chamber and vestry, south porch and bell-cote. A plain round-headed doorway of *c.*1100–1150, now blocked, is in the north wall; it is the only surviving feature of the original church, the nave having been substantially restored in 1868–9 for the 5th earl of Portsmouth.

The church has a six-bay, late 15th-century nave roof with tie beams and wind-braces below the purlins.[114] In 1890 the church was extended to provide a chancel and vestry; it was re-seated in oak, with an oak screen and a Willis organ was installed. The work was carried out by Hicks & Charlewood of Newcastle-upon-Tyne in late decorated

110 BTH, Mary Fraser (BAHS 139).
111 HRO, 57M77/NMS12.
112 HRO, 57M77/NMC74. Cliddesden had 14 members in 1964, 6 members in 1976.
113 HRO, 57M77/NMS98.
114 Pevsner, *North Hampshire*, 226.

Figure 27 *Blocked Norman doorway in a niche in the north wall of St Leonard's church.*

style and funded by William Bradshaw of Audleys Wood, as a memorial to his wife and daughter.[115] The furnishings are Victorian with particularly fine tiles on the chancel floor.

The east window of three lights under a traceried head is in early decorated style; the stained glass from the studio of Charles Kempe, 1890–2, depicts the Crucifixion of Christ. It is dedicated to Elizabeth Isabella Floretta Bradshaw by her mother. Other Kempe windows in the nave show scenes from the Passion whilst on the south side of the chancel St Leonard in his chains, St Augustine, St Stephen and St Alban are portrayed.[116] The west window was restored in its original perpendicular style; glass of 1971 is a memorial to the rector, Arthur Badger (d. 1960) given under the will of his sister, Miss F.E. Badger.[117] It shows the descent of the Holy Spirit in the form of a dove, hovering over the chalice.

Monuments include a tablet to Louis de Luze Simonds, 1916, and his wife Mary Elizabeth, 1930, both of whom were churchwardens and to two former rectors, David Davies, 1841 and Harry Sneyd Mather, 1894. A plaque on the south wall commemorates six lives lost in the First World War and two lives lost in the Second World War. Plate consists of a silver-gilt chalice and cover and a silver paten. The small Nuremburg cup is of 16th-century date engraved with festoons of fruit and husks. The paten bears the inscription 'Ecclesiae Parochi: de Cliddesden Elizab: Mia: Reginolds Vidua D.D., 1702'.[118]

Electric light was installed in 1933 and improvements to heating came when an oil-fired system replaced a coke boiler in 1957.[119] In 1948 repairs were undertaken to the roof and roof timbers as well as internal re-decoration and the installation of an electric blower for the organ. The Norman doorway was uncovered during work on the walls

115 HRO, 15M84/E6/7/11; Pevsner, *North Hampshire*, 226.
116 www.farleighcandoverandwield.org.uk/our-churches/cliddesden-st-leonards/about-our-church/
      (accessed 16 Jun. 2017).
117 HRO, 21M65/91F/10.
118 Braithwaite, *Church Plate*, 98.
119 HRO, 21M65.91F/3; 21M65/91F/7.

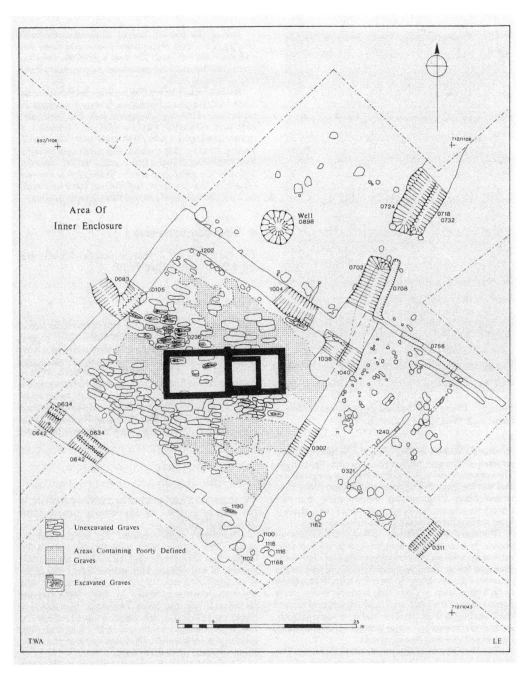

Figure 28 *Plan of the church at Hatch.*

at this time and a tablet fixed to the adjacent wall records the pride parishioners felt in this undertaking which had cost £1,300, entirely raised by voluntary contributions. A new bell was presented by Lady Camrose in 1955. The 5½ cwt bell was cast at the Whitechapel foundry of Mears and Stainbank and replaced a smaller one of *c*.1865.[120]

In the 20th century Rex Paterson of Hatch Warren Farm provided a Garden of Remembrance in the churchyard.[121] The churchyard was classified as a Site of Interest in Nature Conservation and managed as such. A lych-gate, erected as part of the 1890 additions and rebuilt in the early 21st century, formed a welcoming entry to the church.[122]

The Church at Hatch

There was a church at Hatch at the time of the Domesday survey and it is likely that this was the church unearthed by the excavations undertaken prior to development in 1984–6 at Brighton Hill South.[123] These revealed a medieval settlement with a church aligned east–west within a square enclosed cemetery of *c*.900 m². In 2016 the site lay in the north-west corner of an area of open space adjoining Hatch Warren Community Centre.[124] The layout of the church with a nave and a very small chancel suggested a late Saxon origin, confirming the supposition that this was the church recorded in 1086, although the excavation report stressed that a pre-Conquest date could not be proved by the artefactual dating of the site. An enlargement of the chancel was estimated to have occurred during the 12th or 13th centuries. Nine graves were found within the nave of the church, one of which was identified as that of a priest by the presence of his pewter chalice and paten.[125] This grave cut into one containing silver farthings from the reign of Edward I, minted between 1280 and 1300, and so must date between 1280 and *c*.1370 when the church went out of use before its formal abandonment.[126] The church was built of flint and mortar with some chalk, with structural details such as quoins, doors and windows in stone, which was necessarily imported, and to have had a tiled roof at the point at which it fell into disuse.[127] Fragments of window glass and lead tracery found in graves indicated that this was a building of local importance. By 1378 it was in ruins, without a priest, and ceased its existence as a parish church.[128]

120 HRO, 21M65/91F/6.
121 www.farleighcandoverandwield.org.uk (accessed 3 Jun. 2016).
122 www.allsaintschurchdummer.hampshire.org.uk: parish of Farleigh (accessed 1 Oct. 2013).
123 *Domesday*, 120; above, Cliddesden – Introduction, Settlement. Restrictions imposed by the developer prevented removal of floors so that precise dating of the phases of the church was not possible.
124 OS grid ref. SU 606489.
125 Fasham and Keevill, *Brighton Hill*, 81.
126 Ibid., 109.
127 Ibid., 77–9, 146.
128 *Reg. Wykeham* II, 292, 321.

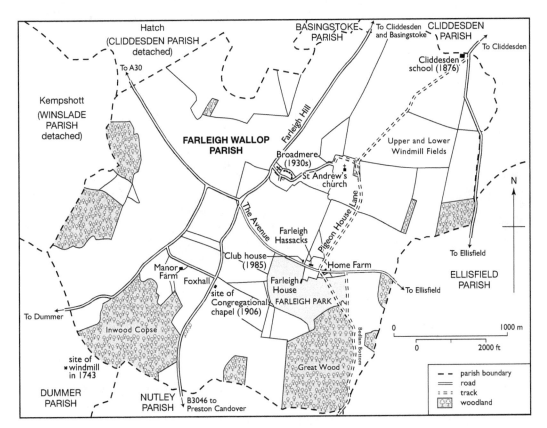

Map 5 *Farleigh Wallop in the 1870s with later structural additions.*

THE PARISH OF FARLEIGH WALLOP lies to the south-west of Cliddesden, further from the centre of Basingstoke yet close to the town's western suburbs. Extensive views of Basingstoke are obtained from a point on the B3046 near the summit of Farleigh Hill. The parish is larger than Cliddesden, consisting of 726 ha. (1,794 a.) of chalk downland and woodland, but its population is much smaller. It has a rural economy based on arable farming and woodland management. Farleigh House, the most prominent building, stands on high ground, and its gardens and park occupy much of the south-west of the parish. The church of St Andrew lies surrounded by fields about a quarter of a mile from the house, and contains many Wallop family memorials.

Figure 29 *The steep-sided valley of Bedlam Bottom.*

Place-names and Farms

The first element in the place-name Farleigh may denote fern or bracken, and the second an area of wood-pasture, similar to those recognised elsewhere on the Hampshire chalk downlands in the late Anglo-Saxon period.[1] The name Farleigh has sometimes caused confusion to historians, as there are several places of the same name in England, including another, Farley Chamberlayne, in Hampshire. The Domesday spelling was Ferlege, and the correct identification in this and later records is confirmed by its location in the Hampshire hundred of Bermondspit. Variant spellings have included Farlege, Farlegh, Farley, Farnlegh and Farlyghe.[2] Confusion was sometimes avoided by the addition of the suffix Mortimer, from the family which held the manor from the late 13th century, and subsequently by the suffix Wallop, from the family which succeeded to it in the 15th century. The inquisition *post mortem* of Sir Henry Wallop (I) in 1599 is the first known document in which Farleigh Mortimer was explicitly equated with Farleigh Wallop, although the name Farleigh Mortimer continued as an alternative to Farleigh

1   Coates, *Place-names*, 76; Banham and Faith, *Anglo-Saxon Farms*, 233.
2   *Domesday*, 122; *Cal. Inq. p.m.* IV, no. 221; *Feudal Aids* II, 313, 344; *Cal. Close 1279–88*, 455; TNA, CP 25/1/205/21.

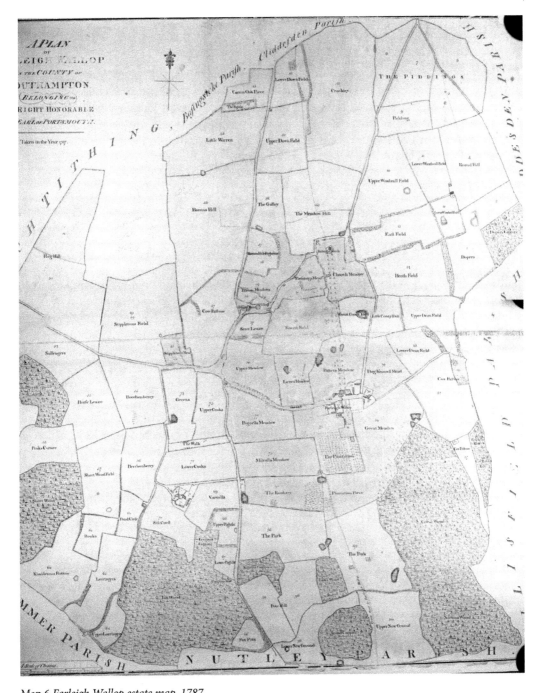

Map 6 *Farleigh Wallop estate map, 1787.*

Wallop until the early 17th century.[3] In this book, the names Farleigh and Farleigh Mortimer have been used for the early history where appropriate, and Farleigh Wallop is used from the 16th century onwards.

Farm names have also varied. Home Farm was sometimes called Park Farm in the 19th century but reverted to its original name of Home Farm in the 20th century.[4] The farmhouse, let separately from the farm, was known as Farleigh Valoynes from 1931 to 1949, reviving the family name of the lords of the manor between the Mortimers and the Wallops in the 16th and 17th centuries.[5] Manor Farm had the variant names of Farleigh Farm and Farleigh Upper Farm in the 19th century.[6] The modern names Home Farm and Manor Farm have been used throughout this book, regardless of those in original documents.

Boundaries and Area

Until 1932 Farleigh Wallop parish was an approximately circular shape, but with some angular sections on its northern side where it abutted Hatch (a detached portion of Cliddesden parish) and the southern end of Basingstoke parish. For a short distance at the south-east corner the parish boundary followed that of Great Wood, adjoining Norton's Wood which lies to the south in Nutley parish. This grouping, perhaps surviving from a larger, now partially cleared area has been characterised as ancient woodland.[7] Apart from this, the boundary did not follow any natural features, not even the deep valley called Bedlam Bottom, a name first recorded in 1851, instead traversing the eastern slope above it.[8] A map of the Farleigh Wallop estate dated 1787 shows that the estate boundary at that time was almost identical with that of the parish in 1842, when the area of the parish was stated as 1,630 a.[9] Between 1851 and 1871 it was 1,675 a., but in the early 1870s it was surveyed at 1,725 a. although there were no intervening boundary changes.[10] The 19th-century boundary was retained as the civil parish boundary after local government reorganisation in 1894 and was kept until 1932, when almost the whole of Hatch was transferred from Cliddesden to Farleigh Wallop, bringing its total area up to 2,420 a.[11]

The M3 motorway, opened in 1971, cut across the enlarged parish. In the same year, 41 ha. (101 a., part of Hatch Warren Farm) were transferred to Basingstoke borough.[12] Apart from this, the north-western boundary was preserved until 1985 when the Farleigh Wallop parish boundary was moved south to the centre of the motorway, reducing the

3   TNA, C 142/256/6; Watney, *Wallop Family* I, xxii.
4   OS 1st edn 1:10,560, Hampshire sheet XXVI, 1875 and later edns; 10th earl of Portsmouth, pers. comm., 2016.
5   HRO, 15M84/3/1/1/113.
6   HRO, 15M84/3/1/1/107; 15M84/E6/1/25.
7   J.L. Phibbs, *Farleigh Park: a Survey of the Landscape* (unpub. rpt, 1989).
8   *Census*, 1851.
9   HRO, 15M84/MP10; 21M65/F7/87/1–2.
10 *Census*, 1851–71; OS 1st edn 1:10,560, Hampshire sheets XVIII, 1877, XXVI, 1875.
11 County of Southampton Review Order: Ministry of Health Order no. 76235; *Census*, 1951.
12 Hampshire (Borough of Basingstoke) Confirmation Order 1971 (Dept of Environment Order no. 3595).

parish area to 726 ha. (1,794 a.).[13] The parish lost a further 9 ha. (22 a.) following a small alteration in the boundary with Cliddesden at some time between 1991 and 2001.[14]

Landscape, Communications and Settlement

Landscape and Geology

Farleigh House stands on a plateau at 650 ft (198 m.) at almost the highest point in the parish, from where the land descends steeply in the east to the valley called Bedlam Bottom before rising again to meet the boundary with Ellisfield to the south east and Cliddesden at 643 ft (196 m.) to the north on the slopes of White Hill. In the north it descends more gently to meet the undulating landscape of Cliddesden and in the south it also descends gradually towards the neighbouring parish of Nutley, while the central high ground continues westwards towards Hatch, since 1971 it has been cut off by the M3 motorway. Farleigh Park occupies the south-western part of the parish and has been a feature of the landscape from the 16th century or earlier.[15] The geology is divided between upper chalk on the lower ground and clay with flints and loam overlying chalk on the higher ground.[16] A pond at Broadmere was man-made, as was a small reservoir supplied from a borehole in the grounds of Farleigh House. This had a double function as an ornamental lake and an emergency water supply.[17] In 2017 arable fields occupied much of the parish, but there were extensive areas of woodland, particularly within Farleigh Park where Great Wood neighboured Nortons Wood in Nutley. In 2017 Farleigh House was surrounded by gardens, which merged into the informal landscape of the park. The church of St Andrew, isolated in grazing land north-north-east of the house was, by the 18th century, approached directly from the house by an avenue of trees.[18] In the 21st century the approach was represented only by the line of a public footpath.

Communications

No public carriers ever served the settlement and the nearest post town during the 18th and 19th centuries was Basingstoke.[19] Only one road of more than local significance passes through the parish, that from Basingstoke via Cliddesden and Preston Candover to Alresford (B3046). This was the route used in the late 16th century by the Farleigh estate bailiffs and servants when making business trips to Basingstoke, Preston Candover and further afield.[20] It was turnpiked in 1795 and disturnpiked, in common with other routes emanating from Basingstoke, in 1871.[21] Two minor roads lead off it in a westerly

13 OS Landranger 1:50,000, sheet 185, rev. 1978; OS Pathfinder 1:25,000, sheet 1224, 1987; *Census*, 1991.
14 Above, Cliddesden – Introduction, Map 3.
15 HRO, 44M69/E5/1.
16 OS Geological maps of England and Wales 1:50,000 series, sheet 284, drift edn.
17 Greta Iddeson, Estate Manager, pers. comm., 2017.
18 HRO, 15M84/MP10.
19 *Parson and Parish*, 39–40; *PO Dir. Hants.*, 1855–67; *Kelly's Dir. Hants.*, 1859–89.
20 HRO, 44M69/E5.
21 HRO, 44M69/G1/156–7; 50M63/C7.

Figure 30 *Farleigh Wallop landscape, looking north towards Basingstoke.*

direction, one towards Dummer and the other towards Kempshott. The latter continues east to Ellisfield, but its first stretch, tree-lined and called The Avenue, functions as part of the formal approach to Farleigh House. A broad track called Pigeon House Lane replaced the earlier, more direct route to the church, beyond which it continued north-east to the point where Cliddesden school stands on the parish boundary. A footpath slightly further west connected the church with Cliddesden village. These roads and tracks carried the daily commerce between Farleigh Wallop and Cliddesden during the centuries in which the two estates were run jointly from Farleigh Wallop.[22] Passengers from Farleigh Wallop could use the station at Cliddesden, two miles distant by footpaths, during the existence of the Basingstoke and Alton Light Railway between 1901 and 1932.[23] In 1927 the Venture Bus Company introduced a service from Basingstoke to the surrounding villages including Farleigh Wallop, and a public bus service has continued ever since, operated by Stagecoach's Cango service between Basingstoke and Alresford in 2016.[24]

Settlement

Early Settlement

A number of prehistoric flint-working sites in Farleigh Wallop lay between those in Cliddesden in the east and Hatch in the west, all located within the clay-with-flints

---

22   Below, Farleigh Wallop – Economic History.
23   Above, Cliddesden – Introduction; Dean and others, *Light Railway*, 87–93.
24   Ibid., 53, 67–8; www3.hants.gov.uk/CANGO (accessed 5 Oct. 2016).

deposits in the higher parts of the parishes. A single Palaeolithic implement was found on Farleigh Hill, along with a large scatter of Neolithic implements, which included many arrowheads, polished and chipped axes and scrapers.[25] A smaller assemblage, consisting of three Mesolithic axe heads and 36 fabricators, was discovered on another slope slightly to the south-east, and a quantity of early Neolithic flint tools came from the plateau west of the road from Basingstoke to Preston Candover (B3046).[26] Two ploughed-out bowl barrows from the early Bronze Age have been recognised, one partly within Inwood Copse in the south of the parish, the other in the north-east. A third possible bowl barrow has been identified south of The Avenue, although it has also been described as a post-medieval windmill mound.[27] Two possible Iron Age sites, one an enclosure of uncertain purpose, and the other a field system, lie close to the boundary with Hatch, and could be associated with the Iron Age features on the plateau there.[28] There is another site, a double-ditched linear feature associated with a circular enclosure close to the southern edge of the parish, identified from an aerial photograph and likely to be late prehistoric.[29] The Roman period is represented by a single brooch found by metal-detecting at Manor Farm.[30] There are no surviving archaeological features from the Roman and Anglo-Saxon periods, and no early church, although settlement was evident in 1086. There were at least 25 households in the manor, of which only three were headed by slaves, which implies that, in contrast to neighbouring Hatch and Cliddesden, the manorial lord kept relatively little land in hand, with the rest distributed in small farms and cottage holdings.[31]

Medieval and Later Settlement and Buildings

By the end of the 13th century, Farleigh had a church with a rector and presumably a rectory house.[32] The rectorial glebe was a field near the church, and remained ecclesiastical property until 1931.[33] The church was the focus of a nucleated settlement, traceable on the ground by earthworks and boundary banks covering an area of nearly 30 a. in the vicinity of the church. It has not been excavated or dated, and the outlines of the individual houses are indistinct, but a broad sunken lane probably marks the village street.[34] An early manor house may have existed in this area, but if so, it was relocated, probably before the end of the 14th century.[35] The settlement was abandoned, and was not re-established near the new house. Depopulation may have been due to the pestilences, as it was at Hatch.[36]

---

25 Hants HER 20272.
26 Hants HER 20304, 20306.
27 Hants HER 20282, 20329, 20284.
28 Hants HER 54547, 55943.
29 Hants HER 36365–6.
30 Hants HER 39538.
31 *Domesday*, 122.
32 Below, Farleigh Wallop – Religious History.
33 HRO, 15M84/2/1/8/1.
34 Hants HER 20298.
35 Below, Farleigh Wallop – Landownership.
36 Above, Cliddesden – Religious History.

Figure 31 *Home Farm House.*

Open fields in Farleigh Wallop had largely disappeared by the late 16th century, and enclosure was complete in the late 18th century.[37] By that time the tenant farms beyond the park limits had been amalgamated, and then divided into larger farms, one of them the demesne farm called Home Farm. At the core of Home Farm is one surviving bay of a modest 17th-century cottage, and the south-west wing has narrow brick dressings consistent with a late 17th- or early 18th-century date. Its knapped flint walls are interspersed with ashlar stone blocks, possibly reused from the original Farleigh House which burnt down in the 1670s and was rebuilt in 1731.[38] Home Farm was extended and altered several times and became a private residence in 1931.[39] Its stables and barns form a large part of the village street scene. One barn has been dated by use of dendrochronology to 1575–6, and is a large, but simple, vernacular building of five bays with side and hip aisles. The roof was partly reconstructed in the 18th century.[40] A large house called Farleigh Hassacks, of which the earliest part dates from the 17th century, may once have been the house associated with the farm.[41] There are very few other buildings in the settlement apart from the Farleigh Wallop club room and Farleigh House behind its high wall.

All the housing stock in Farleigh Wallop belongs to Portsmouth Estates, and much of it was built in the 1930s as part of the 9th earl of Portsmouth's modernisation of the farming estate. A small group of cottages opposite the pond at Broadmere was scarcely a

37   Below, Farleigh Wallop – Economic History.
38   Edward Roberts, pers. comm., 2016; below, Farleigh Wallop – Landownership.
39   HRO, 15M84/3/1/1/113; 15M84/E6/4/108.
40   Hants HER 2261; D. Miles and E. Roberts, 'List 178 Hampshire dendrochronological project – phase 12',
      Vernacular Architecture 37 (2006), 123–4; E. Roberts, 'Hampshire barns c.1300–1675: their dating and
      development', *Historic Farm Buildings Group Rev., Special Edn* 14 (2015), 32.
41   Hants HER 2260; Pevsner, *North Hampshire*, 269.

Figure 32 *The 16th century barn at Home Farm.*

Figure 33 *Farleigh Hassacks.*

hamlet until the 9th earl replaced them with a larger group of semi-detached brick-built houses for estate workers.[42] They form a pleasant if unremarkable group. The few large houses in and near The Avenue, which were built for estate managerial staff in the 1930s, are not visually part of the settlement. In the 19th century there were isolated cottages elsewhere in the parish, but most of these have disappeared and there are no other hamlets.

Population

By 1086 there were at least 25 households in the manor, headed by 15 villeins, seven bordars and three slaves indicating a population of between 100 and 120.[43] This was a relatively large population for rural settlements in Hampshire.[44] Assessments for lay subsidies recorded seven eligible for the tax in 1327 and 11 in 1333.[45] These included Roger de Mortimer, the manorial lord, who was most unlikely to have been resident in Farleigh.[46] The military skills and armour of 11 men were assessed in 1522, although one entry was deleted.[47] The lay subsidy of 1525 named 22 taxpayers but there were only three in 1546 and 1547, and two in 1586.[48] It should be noted that the later lay subsidies are increasingly unreliable as an indication of numbers and wealth of taxpayers.[49] Only three taxpayers with chargeable hearths were recorded in the hearth taxes of 1665, 1673 and 1675, and no houses with unchargeable hearths were recorded in the parish in any of those years.[50] The numbers of communicants in the parish were combined with those of Cliddesden, and were estimated at 108 in 1603 and 110 in 1676.[51] By 1725 the estimated population of the two parishes was 170, which rose to 310 by 1788, the majority being resident in Cliddesden.[52]

The population of Farleigh Wallop as recorded in the 19th- and early 20th-century censuses was very small, significantly smaller than at the time of the Domesday survey, with 50 residents (in 8 houses) in 1801 and reaching a maximum of 118 (in 18 houses) in 1861 before declining to 74 (in 18 houses) in 1921. The number of inhabited houses reached a peak of 24 in 1881 but with 12 fewer occupants than in 1861. By 1931 the population stood at 102. It then rose to 132 as a result of the boundary changes in 1932. Employment on the Farleigh estate increased in the 1930s and by 1951 the parish population had grown to 217 (in 55 houses). The development of Hatch for housing was reflected in the greatly increased population of Farleigh Wallop parish from 185 in 1971 to 1,660 in 1981. Hatch and Farleigh Wallop were constituted an electoral ward (called Farleigh Wallop, later renamed Hatch Warren) of Basingstoke and Deane Borough in

---

42   10th earl of Portsmouth, pers. comm., 2016.
43   *Domesday*, 122.
44   opendomesday.org (accessed 4 Mar. 2016).
45   *Hants Tax 1327*, 41; TNA, E 179/242/15A, rot. 6.
46   Below, Farleigh Wallop – Landownership
47   TNA, E 36/19, 163.
48   TNA, E 179/173/183, rot. 12d.; E 179/174/260, rot. 9; E 179/174/272, rot. 5; *Hants Subsidy 1586*, 54.
49   R.W. Hoyle, *Tudor Taxation Records* (1994), 26–31.
50   *Hearth Tax*, 218; TNA, E 179/176/569, rot. 10; E 179/247/30, rot. 20d.
51   *Dioc. Pop. Returns*, 490; *Compton Census*, 83.
52   *Parson and Parish*, 39, 267.

1985.[53] Development continued throughout the 1980s, and in 1991 Farleigh Wallop ward had a population of 6,688 while Farleigh Wallop parish had a population of 92, which was lower than at any time since the 19th century. By 2001 Farleigh Wallop parish was detached from the ward and joined with the neighbouring parish of Nutley for electoral purposes.[54] There were 86 people in Farleigh Wallop parish in 2001 and 94 in 2010.[55]

53   Basingstoke and Deane (Parishes) Order, 1985; *Census*, 1991.
54   *Census*, 2001.
55   *Census*, 1801–2011; https://www.basingstoke.gov.uk/content/doclib/195.pdf (accessed 26 Sept. 2017).

LANDOWNERSHIP

DOMESDAY BOOK RECORDED A SINGLE manor in Farleigh, in the hundred of Bermondspit. In the 13th century it passed to Joyce de Mortimer and remained in the possession of her descendants for a century. After a period in other hands, Farleigh became part of the extensive estates of the Wallop family. John Wallop (III) was created earl of Portsmouth in 1743, and there have been several other notable members of the family. Farleigh House has been their seat, although not always their home, since the 15th century.

Farleigh Manor to the Late 15th Century

The descent of the overlordship of Farleigh is obscure.[1] It was held from the king in 1086 as it had been in 1066.[2] In 1279 the overlord may have been Reginald Fitz Peter, who held the neighbouring manor of Cliddesden.[3] It is also possible, though it is not recorded among its early holdings, that the overlordship had been granted to the Southwick Priory, Porchester, a royal foundation, some time in the 12th or 13th centuries.[4] In 1486 and 1503 Farleigh was in the overlordship of Southwick Priory,[5] and by 1599 in that of the hundred of Basingstoke.[6]

In 1066 Farleigh was among the numerous estates, mostly spread across the southern England, held by Wulfgifu. She held Farleigh of king Edward and although a woman of that name retained six manors, five in Essex and Cambridgeshire in 1086, Farleigh was not among them.[7] In 1086 Farleigh was held of king William by Sigeric the chamberlain, an Englishman.[8] In 1167 a certain John accounted to the Exchequer for Farleigh.[9] By the 1270s at the latest, the manor was in the hands of Henry of Farleigh, who had been sheriff of Hampshire from 1249 to 1256,[10] and in 1279 Henry passed it to Robert and Joyce de Mortimer.[11] Robert was the son of Hugh de Mortimer (I, d. 1274) of Richard's

---

1   There is no detail of the 1275 overlordships in Bermondspit Hundred in *Rot. Hund.*
2   *Domesday*, 122.
3   Above, Cliddesden – Landownership; below, Farleigh Wallop – Religious History. Robert and Joyce de Mortimer regained the advowson of Farleigh church in 1279 from Reginald Fitz Peter rather than directly from Henry of Farleigh.
4   *VCH Hants* II, 164–8
5   *Cal. Inq. p.m. Hen. VII*, I, no. 187; *Cal. Inq. p.m. Hen. VII*, II, no. 708.
6   TNA, C 142/256/6.
7   *Domesday*, 122; http://domesday.pase.ac.uk/ 'Wulfgifu'(accessed 28 Jan. 2018).
8   *Domesday*, 122. This was his only estate: http://domesday.pase.ac.uk/ 'Sigeric 16' (accessed 26 Jan. 2018).
9   *Pipe R* 1166–7 (PRS 11), 189.
10 Baigent and Millard, *Basingstoke*, 600.
11 *Placit. in Domo Capit. Abbrev.*, 199.

Castle (Herefs.),[12] Joyce (d. 1289/90) was the daughter of William la Zouche (d. 1271/2) and his wife Maud.[13] Joyce was probably related to Henry of Farleigh, though the precise relationship has not been established,[14] and she was a young widow at the time of her marriage to Robert de Mortimer (before 1274).[15] She was a wealthy heiress, part of whose Northamptonshire inheritance from her first husband provoked a dispute which was to last for many generations.[16]

When Robert de Mortimer died in 1287 and Joyce claimed her inheritance, Farleigh was found to be one of the four manors which she possessed in her own right and not as dower.[17] Joyce herself died in 1290, and Farleigh passed, along with her other property, to Hugh de Mortimer (II) of Richard's Castle (Herefs.), her elder son by her marriage to Robert de Mortimer.[18] Dower for Hugh's wife Maud was arranged in 1297 by a process whereby Hugh granted Farleigh and several other manors to William of March, bishop of Bath and Wells, who then regranted them to Hugh and Maud.[19] By this means, Maud was assured of possession of the manors in her own right if Hugh were to predecease her, instead of the standard dower of a third. Hugh did indeed die before her, in 1304, apparently poisoned by Maud herself, although she was pardoned on the intercession of Margaret the queen consort.[20] In 1299–1300, Hugh de Mortimer (II) granted a life interest in Farleigh to John of Droxford (alias Drokensford, d. 1329), from 1309 bishop of Bath and Wells.[21] Maud attempted to regain it in 1306 but the case was adjourned,[22] and she had not succeeded before her own death in 1308.[23] Although John of Droxford did not die until 1329, Farleigh had passed to Roger de Mortimer by 1316.[24] Roger de Mortimer had the highest assessment for the lay subsidies in Farleigh in 1327 and 1333.[25] He is not known as a son of Hugh de Mortimer (I), and his relationship to the Mortimers and his entitlement to Farleigh are not clear.[26]

In 1328 Roger de Mortimer settled the manor and advowson of Farleigh, in which he kept a life interest, on William la Zouche of Ashby.[27] William was the younger brother

12 *Cal. Inq. p.m.* II, no. 132.
13 TNA, CP 25/1/57/77.
14 *Cal. Close* 1279–88, 247. In 1283, in return for service in Wales, Robert de Mortimer was excused from a debt of his own and from debts inherited from his father, father-in-law and Henry of Farleigh.
15 TNA, JUST 1/1223, m. 25. This case, in which many family details were set out, was one of many between the Mortimers and Felicia de Whelton, Joyce's daughter from her first marriage.
16 R.C. Palmer, *The Whilton Dispute, 1264–1380: a Socio-Legal Study of Dispute Settlement in Medieval England* (Princeton, 1984).
17 *Cal. Close* 1279–88, 455.
18 *Cal. Close* 1288–96, 72, 467.
19 *Cal. Pat.* 1292–1301, 304.
20 *Cal. Pat.* 1301–7, 378. L.E. Mitchell, *Portraits of Medieval Women: Family, Marriage and Politics in England, 1225–1350* (New York, 2003), ch. 6, casts doubt on Maud's guilt.
21 *Cal. Inq. p.m.* IV, no. 221.
22 TNA, CP 40/160, rot. 202.
23 *Cal. Inq. p.m.* V, no. 57. Farleigh was not mentioned in her inquisitions. Maud's heirs were her two daughters.
24 *Feudal Aids* II, 313.
25 *Hants Tax 1327*, 289; TNA, E 179/242/15A, rot. 6.
26 TNA, CP 25/1/205/21; *Cal. Pat.* 1330–4, 278. Both documents name him as 'of Richard's Castle' (Herefs.), the title to which may have been disputed with Hugh de Mortimer (II).
27 TNA, CP 25/1/205/21.

of Hugh de Mortimer (II), but had reverted to his mother's family name of Zouche, probably on acquiring the manor of Ashby-de-la-Zouch (Leics.) and other manors from Alan la Zouche, a distant cousin.[28] William la Zouche was created Baron Zouche of Mortimer in 1323.[29] He died in 1337 and his elder son died in 1346, leaving an heir who was underage.[30] In that year Farleigh was held by Robert la Zouche, the younger son of Baron Zouche.[31] He and his wife Margaret were still in possession in 1371[32] but Robert died before 1399, [33] possibly by 1390, when the manor was held by Margaret Illeston. In that year she and her husband Thomas Illeston conveyed it to William Pant, parson of Farleigh church.[34] Margaret was probably Robert la Zouche's widow and she was widowed again by 1391.[35] By the late 14th century the Zouches of Mortimer had no direct heirs[36] and Farleigh passed out of the family which had held it for more than a century and from whom its alternative name of Farleigh Mortimer was derived. It had always been remote from the other Mortimer and Zouche estates.

The descent of Farleigh in the first quarter of the 15th century presents some uncertainties. Although the sale in 1390 was to William Pant 'and his heirs for ever', it was a legal device, and he was not the intended long-term owner. In the 16th century, Sir Nicholas de Valognes[37] was said to have been lord of both Farleigh and Cliddesden.[38] He was active in the late 14th and the early 15th centuries, making appearances in the Basingstoke hundred court between 1386 and 1410 in various capacities, and he obtained a licence for a private chapel for himself and his wife Elizabeth as 'lord of Farleigh' in 1398.[39] He presented a rector to Farleigh church in 1411.[40] His daughter and heir Margaret was said to have married first Sir Thomas Wallop and then William Vachell.[41] William Vachell held Cliddesden in 1428 and presumably acquired Farleigh later, since he presented rectors to Farleigh church in 1448 and 1450.[42] Between the tenures of Sir Nicholas de Valognes and William Vachell, Farleigh was for a time in the hands of Sir John Wintershall of Wintershall and Shalford, Surrey, MP for the county six times between 1401 and 1433. He was recorded as holding Farleigh in 1428 and 1431.[43] He may have acquired it by marriage, possibly to the widow of Sir Nicholas de Valognes.[44]

28   *Complete Peerage* VIII, 228; *Cal. Close* 1318–23, 654–5; *Cal. Inq. p.m.* V, no. 458.

29   *Complete Peerage* VIII, 228.

30   *Cal. Inq. p.m.* VIII, no. 112; *Complete Peerage* VIII, 228.

31   *Feudal Aids* II, 330.

32   TNA, CP 25/1/206/27.

33   *Complete Peerage* VIII, 228.

34   TNA, CP 25/1/207/28.

35   *Cat. Anct. Deeds* II, 525. She was named as 'Margaret Zouche, late the wife of Thomas de Ilkeston' in a demise issued at Farleigh Mortimer.

36   *Complete Peerage* VIII, 228.

37   Variants: Valoignes, Valoynes, Valoines and Valence.

38   W.H. Rylands (ed.), *Pedigrees from the Visitation of Hampshire made by Thomas Benolt, Clarenceulx...* (1913), 25; Berry, *Hants. Gen.*, 41; Watney, *Wallop Family* I, 7.

39   Baigent and Millard, *Basingstoke*, 203, 221, 223, 247, 254; *Reg. Wykeham* II, 482.

40   Reg. Beaufort, f. 88.

41   Berry, *Hants. Gen.*, 41; Watney, *Wallop Family* I, 7. There is no independent proof of either of these marriages, but the subsequent descents of the two manors support them.

42   *Feudal Aids* II, 344; Reg. Waynflete I, ff. 6, 10.

43   *Feudal Aids* II, 344, 364.

44   *Hist. Parl. House of Commons 1386–1421* IV, 879–80.

Farleigh Manor from the Late 15th Century

By the late 15th century, Farleigh, Hatch and Cliddesden were held by John Wallop (I), the son of Margaret de Valognes and Sir Thomas Wallop.[45] The Wallop family originated in the area of the Wallop villages, on the border between Hampshire and Wiltshire, and by the 15th century had expanded their landholdings to include Soberton near Portsmouth. John Wallop (I) was twice sheriff for the county and sat briefly in Parliament.[46] At the time of his death in 1486, he held not only the Hampshire and Wiltshire lands inherited from his grandfather (his father being already dead) but also the manors of Farleigh Mortimer, Cliddesden and Hatch, presumably inherited through his mother after the death of her second husband William Vachell.[47]

His son and heir Richard Wallop (d. 1503) had no children.[48] He was succeeded by his brother Robert, who abandoned a legal career in favour of the family tradition of public office. Between 1509 and 1524 he was sheriff of Hampshire on three occasions and bailiff of Basingstoke on four.[49] In spite of his three marriages, Sir Robert Wallop was also childless.[50] He outlived his brothers, and the estates descended to his nephew Sir John Wallop in 1535.

Sir John (d. 1551), used Farleigh Wallop as his home when in England but was a diplomat and soldier.[51] His first diplomatic expedition was to the Low Countries in 1511, but he is better known for his youthful naval exploits against French coastal towns between 1512 and 1515, first as commander of a series of ships and then of a squadron. He fought for the Portuguese in Morocco against Islamic forces for two years, followed by three years in Ireland and then a renewed command in France in the early 1520s and an appointment as lieutenant of Calais in 1530. In 1532 he was sent as ambassador to Paris, and his next ten years were spent largely in France, culminating in the captaincy of the castle of Guînes within the Calais Pale in 1540.

In 1541 he was recalled to England accused of treason. A professed Catholic, his disapproval of Henry's divorce from Katherine of Aragon had been forgiven, but the charge of treason was part of the political infighting which followed the downfall of Thomas Cromwell. Sir John gave himself up voluntarily for questioning, the offence was pardoned and he was restored to the king's favour and returned to Calais. He died and was buried at Guînes in 1551, although later reburied at Farleigh Wallop.[52]

Although Sir John Wallop was married twice, he had no children, and his brother Oliver succeeded to his estates. Oliver Wallop (d. 1566), knighted in 1547, was sheriff of Hampshire in 1558–9.[53] His estates, including Farleigh, Hatch and Cliddesden, passed to his son Sir Henry Wallop (I), an Elizabethan courtier and diplomat. He was knighted in 1569, and was MP for Southampton in 1572. In 1579 he was appointed under-treasurer

45   Berry, *Hants. Gen.*, 41; Watney, *Wallop Family* I, 7. Baigent and Millard, *Basingstoke*, 291–2.
46   Watney, *Wallop Family* I, x–xxiv.
47   *Cal. Inq. p.m. Hen. VII*, I, no. 187.
48   Watney, *Wallop Family* I, xxiv; *Cal. Inq. p.m. Hen. VII*, II, no. 708.
49   Watney, *Wallop Family* I, xxv–xxvii.
50   TNA, PROB 11/25/347.
51   TNA, PROB 11/34/329.
52   *ODNB*, s.v. Wallop, Sir John (b. before 1492, d. 1551), soldier and diplomat (accessed 11 Nov. 2014).
53   Watney, *Wallop Family* I, xxxv.

for Ireland, where he served for most of the rest of his life. He was granted the lands of the abbey and castle of Enniscorthy in County Wexford where he established a trading community. His Irish lands were added to the Wallop family's hereditary estates. He died in Dublin in 1599, and was buried in St Patrick's cathedral.[54]

Sir Henry Wallop (I) was succeeded by his son Sir Henry Wallop (II), who was more closely involved in English and Hampshire affairs. He sat ten times for Parliament for Hampshire towns but chiefly for the county.[55] His son, Sir Robert Wallop, entered Parliament in 1621 and sat at various times for Hampshire, Andover and Whitchurch. In 1641, he signed the document upholding the privileges of Parliament. Though not a Cromwellian by inclination, he was on the parliamentary side throughout the Civil War, and was a commissioner of the court which tried the king but was not accounted a regicide. He attended only two meetings of the commissioners and two days of the week-long trial, did not sign the death warrant and afterwards claimed that he had tried to help the king. Nevertheless he held public appointments during the Commonwealth, and was granted £10,000 out of the confiscated estates of the marquis of Winchester, his royalist neighbour at Basing.

At the Restoration in 1660 he was expelled from Parliament and arrested for his part in Charles's trial. He petitioned unsuccessfully for a pardon and was imprisoned in the Tower of London. He had to endure the humiliation of being dragged on a sledge to Tyburn with a rope around his neck, on the anniversary of Charles's death sentence. This punishment was intended to happen every year, and he had to undergo it at least twice in spite of his failing health. Sir Robert's estates had been confiscated and were restored to him in 1661 through the intervention of his brother-in-law Thomas Wriothesley, 4th earl of Southampton.[56] His first wife, Anne Wriothesley, died in 1662. The following year he married Mary Lambert, daughter of a parliamentary general, and, following her death, Elizabeth Tompson in 1666.[57] Elizabeth shared his imprisonment until he died in 1667.[58]

Sir Robert Wallop was succeeded by his son Henry (d. 1679). A confirmed royalist, he was elected to the first post-Restoration Parliament. Shortly afterwards he was made colonel of a regiment in the Hampshire militia, a title by which he was subsequently known.[59] Colonel Wallop's widow, Dorothy Bluett, outlived him by more than twenty years.[60] The next three heirs were their sons Henry Wallop (d. 1691), John Wallop (II, d. 1695) and John's son, Bluett Wallop (d. 1707).[61]

The early death of Bluett Wallop, aged just 23, meant that his brother John Wallop (III) succeeded to the family estates while still a schoolboy. In 1708, John (III) embarked on an extended tour of Europe, where he developed an interest in art and architecture. On his return, he stood for Parliament in 1713 but was not elected until 1715, in the Whig administration of Sir Robert Walpole. When the Whigs split in 1717 Wallop remained loyal to the ruling faction led by Lord Sunderland. Walpole was restored to

54   ODNB, s.v. Wallop, Sir Henry (c.1531–1599), administrator and member of parliament (accessed 11 Nov. 2014).
55   Watney, *Wallop Family* I, xlvi–xlviii.
56   ODNB, s.v. Wallop, Robert (1601–67), politician (accessed 11 Nov. 2014); *Cal. SP Dom.* 1661–2, 70, 94.
57   www.familysearch.org: registers of All Hallows, Barking, Essex (accessed 18 Apr. 2006).
58   Watney, *Wallop Family* I, liii.
59   Ibid. I, liv.
60   HRO, 44M69/F3/6.
61   TNA, PROB 4/2942; PROB 11/429/209; Watney, *Wallop Family* I, lv–lvi.

Figure 34 *John Wallop,
1st earl of Portsmouth by
Sir Joshua Reynolds.*

power in 1720 and John (III) had to give up his position as a lord of the Treasury, but was created Baron Wallop and viscount Lymington. He took little part in politics during the next ten years, but in the 1730s received a string of Hampshire appointments, from the lord lieutenancy of the county to the governorship of the Isle of Wight. All of these were terminated when Walpole resigned in 1742, but Wallop was created earl of Portsmouth in the following year.[62]

His eldest son John Wallop (IV) (d. 1749) married Catherine Conduitt, a great-niece of Sir Isaac Newton, in 1740.[63] The connection with Newton was a source of pride in the family, which retained many of his papers, and 'Isaac' and 'Newton' were used as first names for several generations afterwards. In consequence of Viscount Lymington's early death, John Wallop (III), 1st earl of Portsmouth was succeeded in 1762 by his eldest grandson, John Wallop (V).[64] His wife was Urania, daughter of Coulson Fellowes, who

62   *ODNB*, s.v. Wallop, John, first earl of Portsmouth (1690–1762), politician (accessed 19 Nov. 2014).
63   Watney, *Wallop Family* I, lix–lx.
64   TNA, PROB 11/882/235.

was MP for Huntingdon in the mid 18th century and heir to the estate of Eggesford in north Devon. This descended through Urania, countess of Portsmouth, to her second son Newton on condition that he used Fellowes as his surname.[65]

The 2nd earl of Portsmouth led a more private life than his predecessors and there was a problem with his eldest son, John Charles Wallop, who had a mental disability which became apparent early in his life. When it finally became clear that he would not be capable of running the estates when the time came, trustees were appointed on his behalf.[66] He became 3rd earl of Portsmouth on the death of his father in 1797, and contracted two marriages, the second of which was challenged by his brothers. A commission of inquiry in 1823 found him insane and lengthy legal proceedings ensued, as a result of which the marriage was annulled in 1828.[67] The earl lived until 1853, by which time his brother Newton Fellowes Wallop was 81 and had less than a year in which to enjoy his inheritance as 4th earl of Portsmouth. The 4th earl's public career was divided between Hampshire and Devon, and he sat for Andover in four parliaments between 1802 and 1820, and for North Devon twice in the 1830s.[68] Nine children resulted from his two marriages but only one son, Isaac Newton Fellowes, survived, becoming the 5th earl of Portsmouth in 1854. On succession he resumed the family name of Wallop. The 5th earl's political views were Liberal, and as an Irish landlord he advised Gladstone on the question of Irish land reform. In gratitude Gladstone offered him first a marquisate and then the Garter, but both offers were declined.[69]

Newton Wallop succeeded his father as 6th earl of Portsmouth in 1891. He too was a Liberal, and sat as MP for North Devon until his succession to the title. He remained active in politics, serving as Under-Secretary for War between 1905 and 1908. Some of the Wallop estates, including those in Ireland, were sold in the early 20th century but not Farleigh Wallop or Cliddesden. The 6th earl died in 1917 and was outlived for 18 years by his widow Beatrice.[70] They were childless and John Fellowes Wallop (d. 1925) succeeded to his brother's title as 7th earl of Portsmouth, but not to the estates which Beatrice, countess of Portsmouth, held for life. The 7th earl travelled and spent time as private secretary to the governor of Tasmania. In later years he devoted himself to his Devonshire garden and to service on the Devonshire County Council.[71] His heir, and 8th earl of Portsmouth, was his younger brother, Oliver Henry Wallop. Oliver Wallop had emigrated as a young man to the United States, where he made a successful career as a rancher and sat for a time in the Wyoming State Legislature.[72] On succeeding to his title, he remained in the USA and prepared his elder son Gerard Vernon Wallop for his future inheritance by educating him at Winchester College.[73]

After service in the First World War, Gerard Wallop finished his education at Balliol College, Oxford, and then, at the Oxford School of Agriculture, began to acquire

65 E.H. Fellowes, *The Family and Descendants of William Fellowes of Eggesford* (Windsor, 1910), 23.
66 *A Genuine Report of the Proceedings on the Portsmouth Case* (1823), 7.
67 TNA, C 211/20/P159; Watney, *Wallop Family* I, lxiv.
68 Ibid. I, lxv–lxvii.
69 HRO, 15M84/5/7/5.
70 Watney, *Wallop Family* I, lxx.
71 Ibid. I, lxxi.
72 S. Morton, *Where the Rivers Run North* (Sheridan, Wyoming, 2007).
73 *ODNB*, s.v. Wallop, Gerard Vernon ninth earl of Portsmouth (1898–1984), politician and environmentalist (accessed 25 Nov. 2014).

expertise in organic farming. The deaths of his uncle in 1925 and father in 1943 respectively brought him the titles of viscount Lymington and 9th earl of Portsmouth. He inherited the family estates in 1935 on the death of his aunt Beatrice. He embarked on a Conservative political career as MP for Basingstoke in 1929, but resigned in 1934. From 1930 he directed the English Mistery, a secretive, quasi-military organisation stressing 'back to the land', English nationalism, and monarchism, and from 1936 he directed its successor, the English Array. In this and other political activities in the second half of the 1930s Gerard Wallop combined far-Right nationalism with criticism of industrial farming, while promoting organic methods.[74] The combination of death duties and the economic depression of the 1930s caused him to rationalise his assets by sales of land and to concentrate on his estates near Basingstoke, and during the Second World War he was vice-chair of Hampshire's War Agriculture Executive Committee.[75] He served from 1947–9 as president of the Country Landowners' Association and he was a prominent member of the Soil Association and other agricultural bodies. In 1948 he visited Kenya, where he bought the first of several estates, and moved there permanently in 1950. He continued to work for agricultural reform there, serving on the Kenyan Legislative Council, and to sit on environmental committees, even after his farms were nationalised following Kenyan independence in 1963.[76] Ill-health forced his eventual return to Farleigh Wallop, where he died in 1984.

The 9th earl's elder son, Oliver Kintzing Wallop, did not inherit the family estates. The taxes which had adversely affected his father's inheritance resulted in the adoption of a scheme which effectively cut him out of the succession. In 1950 he took up farming with his father in Kenya, but the altitude did not suit him and he did not share his father's interest in agriculture. He tried many different occupations and countries before finally settling in England in 1965. He died shortly before his father, and his son Quentin Gerard Carew Wallop became the 10th earl of Portsmouth in 1984. He moved permanently to the Farleigh estate in 1978, 28 years after the departure of the 9th earl. The estate finances were managed in the interim by trustees, who made astute sales of land for building as the development of Basingstoke advanced. Lord Portsmouth was able to undertake a major programme of modernisation on the Farleigh estate, including the restoration of Farleigh House, which was financed in part by the sale of 300 a. at Hatch Warren Farm.[77] In 2017 the 10th earl's son Oliver Henry Rufus Wallop, viscount Lymington was his heir.

Farleigh House

There is no firm evidence for an early manor house at Farleigh, although there may have been one in the 13th century when Henry of Farleigh held the manor.[78] If so, it was probably part of a complex which included the church, rectory and surrounding

74 Conford, 'Organic society', passim.
75 10th earl of Portsmouth, pers. comm., 2016; below, Farleigh Wallop – Economic History.
76 Wallop, *Knot of Roots.*
77 10th earl of Portsmouth, pers. comm., 2016.
78 Nothing is known of Sir William de Valognes, who was said to have a seat at Farleigh temp. Henry III, contrary to J. Stevens, *A Parochial History of St Mary Bourne* (1888) 157, cited in *VCH Hants* III, 366.

Figures 35 and 36 *Above, Farleigh House, west front in 1937 and below, Farleigh House, east front in 2007.*

settlement.[79] Margaret la Zouche issued a demise at Farleigh in 1391 and must have been temporarily resident.[80] Seven years later, Nicholas de Valognes, then lord of Farleigh, obtained a licence for a private chapel for himself and his wife Elizabeth.[81] A relocation of the house to its present site would account for the isolation of the church. From the time of John Wallop (I) onwards, Farleigh House was the Wallop family's most enduring home, though not always the most used, and many family members chose to be buried in the church or graveyard despite spending their lives elsewhere. Farleigh Park, created at an unknown date, and covering *c.*50 a. in 2017, is situated to the south of the house and north of Great Wood. It can be identified on Saxton's map of *c.*1575 and shown as enclosed within a pale though recorded as used for pasture shortly afterwards.[82]

The inventory taken on the death of Sir Oliver Wallop in 1566 shows that Farleigh House was large but typically medieval, with a hall, a gallery, ten chambers and the normal range of service rooms. It also had an armoury, a chapel and a gatehouse.[83] Sir Oliver's son, Sir Henry Wallop (I), was absent in Ireland for long periods but he authorised repairs and rebuilding between 1581 and 1584, some of which were so extensive that they amounted to a remodelling of the house.[84] An upper floor was inserted into the open hall, the service rooms were demolished and rebuilt on a larger scale, and the stable was rebuilt, the total building costs amounting to over £1,100. The house was completely refurnished and considerable amounts were also spent on the garden and the park. During this period the house was occupied intermittently by two of Sir Henry's sons, who were still in education, and by his friends and associates. Sir Henry and his wife Katharine were in residence from 1589 to 1595 and entertained Elizabeth I and her court briefly in 1591.[85] Even with the alterations of the previous decade, Farleigh was not one of the very large houses which some of Elizabeth's hosts built for her visits and it is probable that temporary buildings or tents were erected for the occasion.[86]

The house burnt down, although sources differ as to the date. A plaque in the south-west wall of the present house reads 'Conflagrata 1661' but Colonel Henry Wallop was taxed on 17 hearths in Farleigh Wallop in 1665 and 1673, and on 16 hearths in 1675, which implies that his house was substantial and habitable for longer than was once thought.[87] The destruction is confirmed by a probate inventory taken in 1691.[88] Farleigh House had a porter's lodge with rooms on two floors, a stable with chambers over it, a dairy and other outhouses, but no other rooms were listed, implying that the main house was unoccupied. The stable-block, now offices, appears to have survived the fire, and parts of some walls and two mullioned windows are preserved in the present house.[89]

---

79   Above, Farleigh Wallop – Introduction.
80   *Cat. Anct. Deeds* II, 525.
81   *Reg. Wykeham* II, 482.
82   http://www.geog.port.ac.uk/webmap/hantsmap/hantsmap/saxton1/sax1smaf.htm (accessed 24 Oct. 2017); below, Farleigh Wallop – Economic History.
83   HRO, 21M65/D2/18.
84   HRO, 44M69/E5/1.
85   J. Stevenson (ed.), *Correspondence of Sir Henry Unton* (1847), nos. 42–3.
86   J. Osborne, *Entertaining Elizabeth I: the Progresses and Great Houses of her Time* (1989), 88–92; A. Weir, *Elizabeth the Queen* (1998), 262–8.
87   *Hearth Tax*, 218; TNA, E 179/176/569, rot. 10; E 179/247/30, rot. 20d.
88   TNA, PROB 4/2942.
89   Pevsner, *North Hampshire*, 269; HER 993.

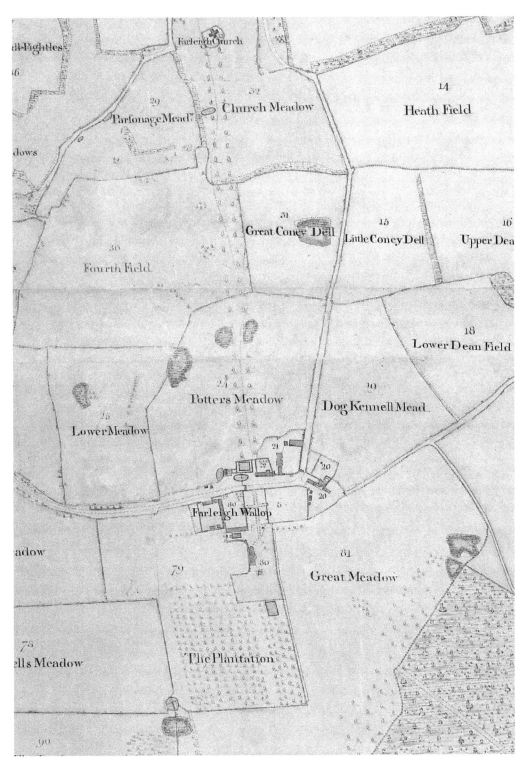

Map 7 *Farleigh House and its surroundings in 1787.*

The family had another Hampshire home, Hurstbourne Park, to which they moved after the fire, although many members of the family continued to identify themselves as 'of Farleigh' when making their wills.

Farleigh House was restored in 1731 as part of a larger building programme by John Wallop (III).[90] It has been suggested that he intended it to be a home for his eldest son, or that it was a hunting lodge.[91] It is true that the house was on the small scale suitable for a hunting lodge, but there was better hunting at Hurstbourne Park and his son was only 13 in 1731. Whatever he may have intended, John Wallop did not occupy Farleigh House, which was let to tenants almost immediately.[92] The park was maintained and the estate managed,[93] but the family did not return there, preferring Hurstbourne Park and Eggesford throughout the 18th and 19th centuries.[94] For a time, the 6th earl of Portsmouth considered selling the Farleigh estate, but decided against it, and the house continued to be let until the mid 1930s.[95]

When Gerard Wallop decided to reoccupy Farleigh House himself in the 1920s, he found it in a bad state. The east front was relatively unaltered, but the west front had been disfigured with various accretions which spoilt the entrance. All these were stripped away and replaced with new rooms on two floors and with a new service wing, virtually doubling the size of the house and creating a harmonious façade. The work, to the designs of H.S. Goodhart-Rendel, was finished in 1937.[96] The house is mainly of two storeys with an attic and basement. The east front has two bays on either side of a projecting angular centrepiece, which has a carved coat of arms above the French window. The west front, which is wider than the east, has a tall projecting centrepiece between two bays, on either side of which are short projecting three-bay wings and two outer single-storey one-bay extensions terminated by piers. The west front is the main entrance to the house, signalled by the prominent coat of arms above the roof of the centrepiece. The walls are of flint with stone dressings, apart from the centrepiece of the east front, which is of fine ashlar, and the roofs are of slate. Inside, the central rooms of the east front are octagonal and give wide views over a lawn and the park. Staircases and doors date from the 1731 rebuilding, and a small room with 17th-century panelling and a stone fireplace survives from the previous house on the site.[97]

During the Second World War the 9th earl and his wife shared the house with agricultural students, evacuees and recuperating officers. Farleigh House was unoccupied for some time after the earl moved to Kenya, and was leased in 1954 to become Farleigh House School. When the lease expired in 1983, the school was relocated to Redrice near Andover, and Quentin Wallop, 10th earl of Portsmouth regained possession. The house, which had suffered during the school's occupation, needed extensive renovation which

90   Pevsner, *North Hampshire*, 268–9; A.M. Deveson, 'Hurstbourne Park: image and reality', *Proc. Hants F.C.* 59 (2004), 198–201.

91   C. Hussey, 'Farleigh House, Hampshire', *Country Life* (1941), 476; G. Worsley, 'Farleigh House, Hampshire', *Country Life* (1994), 62.

92   HRO, 15M84/3/1/1/94.

93   HRO, 15M84/MP10.

94   A.M. Deveson, *En Suivant la Vérité: a History of the Earls of Portsmouth and the Wallop Family* (Farleigh Wallop, 2008), 34–41.

95   HRO, 15M84/3/1/3/5, 15M84/3/1/1/104, 108–9, 692.

96   H.S. Goodhart-Rendel, 'Farleigh House, near Basingstoke, Hampshire', *The Builder* 154 (1938), 67–9.

97   NHLE, no. 1339532 Farleigh House (accessed 10 Aug. 2017).

was completed in 1990, and the gardens were completely redesigned by Georgia Langton during the following years.[98] Flower gardens lie on one side of the east front and wooded walks lead to a man-made lake on the other, while lawns and a cricket pitch frame the western approach from the main gateway. In 2015 the house underwent further modernisation, and in 2016 was no longer a family home but a business enterprise.[99]

98   10th earl of Portsmouth, pers. comm., 2016.
99   Below, Farleigh Wallop – Economic History.

ECONOMIC HISTORY

FARLEIGH WALLOP HAS BEEN, AND in 2017 still was, dominated by agriculture. The parish forms the core of the Farleigh Wallop estate and consists of Farleigh House, former home of the earls of Portsmouth and centre of the estate management, two farms and houses for estate staff. In the 21st century some houses were let to people from outside the parish but otherwise all employment and economic activity related to the estate. Boundary changes in the 20th century meant that between 1932 and 1985 Hatch was part of the parish, extending its size and population and increasing the number of farms from two to three. The land is largely arable with some permanent pasture and significant areas of woodland in the south and south-west of the parish.

The Agricultural Landscape

In 1086 Farleigh was said to have 16 a. of demesne meadow, an unusual but not unique occurrence in the parishes of the high chalklands south of Basingstoke.[1] It also had arable land and woodland for fencing.[2] In the late 16th century at least one large open field remained, but other smaller fields were enclosed.[3] The parish was divided between woodland, arable and grazing land (meadow and pasture) in the 18th and 19th centuries, the grazing land being concentrated around the church and Farleigh House, and the woodland chiefly on the southern and western perimeter, which was perhaps once even more densely wooded.[4] In 1841 the parish was described as 'somewhat inferior to Cliddesden which it adjoins. It contains a large proportion of grass land part of which is very useful upland meadow. The mode of occupation is also similar'.[5] The following year the acreages were given as 1,107 a. of arable, 250 a. of meadow or pasture, 244 a. of woodland, 9 a. of glebe (a meadow) and 20 a. of waste, a total of 1,630 a.[6] In 1872 the arable had increased to 1,140 a. and the woodland to 280 a., but pasture had decreased to 206 a., the remaining acres having been classified as the ornamental ground in Farleigh Park.[7]

In 2016 Farleigh Wallop remained an agricultural parish, with similar land use as in the 19th century, and the woodland is closely managed as part of the wider Portsmouth

1 H.C. Darby and E.M.J. Campbell (eds), *Domesday Geography of South-east England* (Cambridge, 1962), 340.
2 *Domesday,* 122.
3 Below, Estate Management and Farming before 1600.
4 HRO, 15M84/MP10; 21M65/F7/87/2.
5 TNA, IR 18/8984.
6 HRO, 21M65/F7/87/1.
7 OS, *Book of Reference to the Plan of the Parish of Farleigh Wallop* (1872).

Estates. Mixed broadleaf plantings date from the 1860s, with an equal amount of conifer plantation dating from the 1960s, when it was leased by the Forestry Commission. The lease was bought back in 1986 and in 2016, the conifers were gradually being replaced with broadleaf woodlands in order to enhance the commercial sporting value of the Farleigh Shoot, a pheasant shooting operation.[8]

Estate Management and Farming before 1600

In 1086 Farleigh manor had arable land for eight ploughteams, equating to perhaps 800–960 a. The value to the lord, including tenants' rents, was £6, a reduction from £8 in 1066. The one-plough, *c*.120 a.demesne was worked by three slaves, and six tenant ploughs were shared among 15 villeins and seven bordars.[9] Land for eight ploughteams – perhaps representing *c*.880 – *c*.1,000 a. – but only seven working teams suggests a contraction of the cultivated area and may account for the fall in value after the Conquest. The tenant population was concentrated in the area near the church, but when the settlement was abandoned and Farleigh House became the permanent estate centre, the number of tenancies probably diminished.[10]

Documented disputes involving the lord of Farleigh, John Wallop (I) provide evidence of large medieval sheep flocks. Several times in the 1450s he and his men entered the common fields of Basingstoke and by various means tried to prevent the townspeople from grazing their cattle there. This was both a trespass and an attempt to convert some of the Basingstoke downland to sheep pasture, and in 1463 he was fined for persistent efforts to trespass with a large flock of 700 sheep, which were presumably from one of his home manors of Farleigh or Cliddesden.[11] A short run of accounts for the late 16th century shows an established system of sheep-with-corn husbandry. These consolidated accounts were presented by William Jephson and William Wallop for most of the decade beginning in 1579, during the absence of Sir Henry Wallop (I) on government business in Ireland.[12] William Wallop was Sir Henry's brother, and William Jephson of Froyle was a member of a Hampshire gentry family. They acted as stewards for the management of the estates, and had oversight of the bailiffs of individual manors, whose own accounts were incorporated into the records of the annual audit. The estate accounts always began with the income from Farleigh Wallop, where the audit was held, followed by the income from the other manors, but the expenses were mainly for Farleigh Wallop and Cliddesden.

For the accounting year 1587–8 there is a single account for Farleigh Wallop, Hatch and Cliddesden, which combines the records of three 'bailiffs and servants' – William Hayman (who died during the year), William Prince (who joined the team at the beginning of the year) and John Buckland. There is also the separate account of William Prince.[13] From these and the other accounts, it appears that one bailiff (sometimes

8   Oliver Wallop, viscount Lymington, pers. comm., 2016.
9   *Domesday*, 122.
10   Above, Farleigh Wallop – Introduction.
11   Baigent and Millard, *Basingstoke*, 291–303.
12   HRO, 44M69/E5/1, 3–4.
13   HRO, 44M69/E5/2, 7.

called 'bailiff of the husbandry') had responsibility for Farleigh Wallop and the warren at Hatch, but Cliddesden had no specific bailiff. The demesne farm at Cliddesden was leased to William Prince throughout the period, and his and other rents and receipts were accounted for by a farmer acting as rent-collector. After Hayman's death, Prince took over some of his duties in Farleigh Wallop, and acted jointly with John Buckland during that year and the next. Buckland succeeded William Hayman as bailiff of Farleigh Wallop and of 'the husbandry' but there is no clear differentiation between his duties and those of William Prince during those two years, with both men (and Hayman, during his life) handling similar business for both Farleigh Wallop and Cliddesden. John Buckland was in day-to-day financial control, and in charge of the maintenance of the farm staff.[14] Other officers and servants included the keeper of Farleigh House and his wife, a park-keeper and his assistant and four shepherds. Apart from one short-term lease, Farleigh Wallop was entirely in hand at this period. Work on the demesne was done by a combination of paid employees, piece work, day labour and some outside contractors for specialist work such as the smith at Basingstoke. Some workers paid for their own food, others ate at the Farleigh farm as part of their wages. In 1589 there were ten in the household but the number of workers could go up to 20 men when occasion demanded, and around 24 women, who were paid for weeding.[15]

The accounts are not laid out in the regular form of medieval accounts, and do not have complete records of grain and livestock, but some inferences can be made from payments to workers and from the more detailed account of the three bailiffs in the accounting year 1587–8. Open and enclosed fields coexisted and there was at least one large open field, called Sellinger, as well as a number of smaller ones. Some of the field names such as Cooks Closes and Broadmere Mead suggest enclosure, and there were payments for making and repairing hedges. The enclosed fields were predominantly meadows, producing crops of grass and hay, and barley and oats were grown on the uplands. The area under direct demesne cultivation was small, perhaps about 15 per cent of the total area of the two manors, excluding Hatch. The rest was occupied by freeholds and leaseholds, woodland, downland and Farleigh Park, part of which was used for hay and grass. Evidence for sheep numbers is for the whole estate, with no differentiation between the separate manors suggesting that the estate was managed as a single entity. The receipts from sales of stock and skins in 1587–8 imply that a three-flock flock of about 850 ewes and 600 wethers was kept, and that there was a five-year cycle for the replacement of old ewes and wethers. About 800 lambs, born in March or April, would survive until weaning in June or July. One third of these were sold at Michaelmas, and the rest kept to replace the old ewes and wethers, or to be sold as shearlings the next Michaelmas.[16] There was a demesne herd of 40 cows, 32 for milking and eight heifers. Bull calves were killed at about five weeks old to provide veal for the aristocratic household, and the bailiff had his own milking herd.[17] This glimpse of the agricultural system in Farleigh Wallop in the late 16th century is consistent with that found on other parts of the Hampshire chalklands, that is, large flocks of sheep supporting a three-

14   HRO, 44M69/E5/5.
15   HRO, 44M69/E5/5, 7.
16   Gavin Bowie, pers. comm., 2016.
17   HRO, 44M69/E5/5.

course rotation of wheat and barley, with small amounts of oats, peas and vetches grown for animal feed.[18]

Testamentary evidence before 1600 is very limited, but confirms that sheep were the main livestock.[19] Three of the surviving five wills were made by members of the Wallop family, of whom only two mentioned livestock. Sir Robert Wallop (d. 1535) bequeathed 100 ewes to Farleigh church and 50 ewes to the church at Cliddesden, presumably from his flocks grazed in those parishes.[20] The inventory of Sir Oliver Wallop (d. 1566), a soldier rather than a farmer, recorded 332 sheep, nine cows and a bull and three geldings, no crops but evidence of brewing. The value of the inventory amounted to £386 2s. 2d., his wealth arising from wide and disparate sources and as such cannot be used to judge the prosperity of farming in the parish.[21] The wills of the two non-Wallop testators included bequests of a few sheep, a cow, a bullock, malt and barley with provision made for their families, suggesting a comfortable lifestyle and income.[22]

Estate Management 1600–1920

There were no landowners in Farleigh Wallop other than the Wallop family, who were generally absentee landlords for most of the 17th, 18th and 19th centuries. The estate was run from the family residence at Hurstbourne Park, 18 miles to the west, by stewards, trustees or land agents, and successive landowners did not take a personal interest in management, apart from occasionally signing leases, during these years. There are no records of formal enclosure at Farleigh Wallop, and all the fields were enclosed by informal means by the late 18th century.[23] Farms were identified by the names of tenants, and there was some fluidity in farm boundaries until the 19th century. By 1842 at the latest, the land was divided mainly between two farms – the Farleigh home farm, with its farmhouse close to the mansion, and Manor Farm centred in the west of the parish. The remaining fields were allocated to Manor Farm in Cliddesden.[24]

Conditions laid down in leases dating from the 17th and 18th centuries demonstrate increasing strictness about upkeep of pasture, manuring, crop rotation and fallow. On this relatively poor land, the usual rotation of winter wheat, spring barley and oats with grass leys of two years' duration was operated. Sheep numbers were not initially stipulated, the only condition being that they should be penned and folded at night, but by the end of the 18th century the leases were specific about the numbers of sheep and lambs to be kept.[25] A lease dated 1833, just before the introduction of artificial fertilisers, is a late example of the local low-input mixed farming system, with a low

18   Bowie, 'Farming practices', 136–44.
19   Farleigh Wallop probate material: https://www.victoriacountyhistory.ac.uk/explore/items/farleigh-
     wallop-probate-material-1521-1600 (accessed 26 Jan. 2017).
20   TNA, PROB 11/25/347.
21   HRO, 21M65/D2/18.
22   HRO, 1535B/28; 1588A/044; below, Farleigh Wallop – Social History.
23   HRO, 15M84/MP10.
24   HRO, 21M65/F7/87/1–2.
25   HRO, 15M84/3/1/1/88; 15M84/3/1/1/103, 105–6.

sheep-to-acreage ratio and the usual five-course crop rotation.[26] Even more demanding
conditions, incorporating root crops and separate fields of sainfoin, were imposed as the
19th century advanced, and small acreages of pulses and vetch were sometimes allowed.[27]
Stipulations that farms were to be worked 'according to the rules of good husbandry,
used and approved in the County of Hants' or 'in the neighbourhood' demonstrate
that estate management was keeping pace with contemporary developments in arable
farming. Leasing of the estate farms, for variable terms and constantly rising annual
rents, was the norm throughout the 19th century, although woodland was kept in hand
for shooting, or let with the mansion.[28]

Tenant Farming 1600–1920

A varied picture of farming in the 17th century is provided by the surviving 13 wills and
four inventories that include those of six yeomen, two husbandmen and a brewer.[29] The
value of the inventories amounts to £803, and varies between £26 and £357, an average of
£114. Livestock consisted of sheep and cattle but the only indication of crops is of barley,
through the presence of the brewer and the recorded ownership of a malt mill.[30] Robert
Tilborow, a yeoman farmer, had six stalls of bees.[31]

The Hankins were a farming family in the 18th century. Richard Hankin leased land
near Farleigh church in 1728, and was succeeded by Richard Hankin the younger and
then by William Hankin senior and junior.[32] The farm was not always well cultivated;
in 1762, it was said to be 'out of tillages'.[33] The land leased by William Hankin in 1774
included fields that were to become part of Home Farm. An advertisement of 1775
indicated that Farmer Hankin would show viewers around Farleigh House on request,
suggesting that he was living nearby.[34]

In 1841 sheep were the main livestock and included 900 ewes with lambs and 300
tegs. The 1,200 fleeces were valued at £184 and lambs at 12s. 6d. a head. Cows, pigs
and poultry were kept for domestic use only. A large acreage of crops was devoted to
turnips (747 a.), well suited to the shallow soil, with wheat and barley grown in equal
amounts (218 a. each), as well as sainfoin, seeds depastured and 74 a. of land left fallow
after rye and tares.[35] The population of the parish in the mid 19th century included two
farmers, agricultural labourers, carters, a woodman, suggesting active management
of the Great Wood and Inwood Copse to the south and west of Farleigh Park, and a
gamekeeper. William Box farmed at Home Farm where he had 400 a. and employed
27 labourers, six carters or carter boys and one nag boy. The carters and nag boy were

---

26   HRO, 15M84/3/1/1/107/1.
27   HRO, 15M84/3/1/1/107/1–2; 15M84/E6/1/25–6.
28   HRO, 21M65/F7/87/1–2; 15M84/3/1/1/108–9.
29   Farleigh Wallop probate material: https://www.victoriacountyhistory.ac.uk/explore/items/farleigh-
     wallop-probate-material-1521-1600.
30   HRO, 1649A/36; 1661A/110.
31   HRO, 1668B/56.
32   HRO, 15M84/3/1/1/35, 91, 98, 100, 103.
33   HRO, 15M84/3/1/100, attached endorsement, 1762.
34   *St James's Chron.*, May 30–Jun. 1, 1775.
35   TNA, IR 18/8984.

hired annually as servants in husbandry and lived in the farm house. At Manor Farm, Robert Brown farmed 550 a. with 15 labourers, four carters, three agricultural labourers, and five servants hired as servants in husbandry. By 1861 both farmers also employed a shepherd and a groom and William Box had reduced the very high number of workers to a total of 20. In contrast to Cliddesden, there were no servants in husbandry by 1871, all employees were non-resident.[36] At the start of the 20th century, the number of sheep kept in the parish had reduced to 400 from just over 900 in 1866, and in the same period cattle had increased from 17 to 92 suggesting that sheep farming was no longer profitable.[37]

Estate Management 1920–2016

Radical change in management began in the early 1920s, when Gerard Vernon Wallop finished his education at the Oxford School of Agriculture, and, knowing that he would eventually inherit the Portsmouth estates, began to manage Farleigh Wallop himself. He found the estates run down, with 'an obsolescent farming system and no policy for the future'.[38] He moved the estate centre back to Farleigh Wallop from Hurstbourne Park, introduced the organic methods for which he was a lifelong advocate, and employed the latest practices and technology in livestock and arable farming, which returned the estate to profitability. He was thus able to fund an extensive programme of investment in new farm buildings, staff houses and cottages, a shop, a community clubhouse and a piped water distribution system. As a result, the Farleigh estate became a showcase, frequently visited by agriculturalists from both home and abroad.[39]

Gerard Wallop became the 9th earl of Portsmouth in 1943.[40] He was an influential writer and speaker on agriculture, and was ahead of his time in warning of the dangers of arable monoculture and the indiscriminate use of chemicals in farming. His books, particularly *Famine in England* and *Alternative to Death*, published in 1938 and 1943 respectively, sealed his reputation as an expert on organic agriculture. He was as much concerned for the people who worked the land as for the land itself, and was one of an international group of thinkers who promoted traditional agricultural methods and values. This group coalesced into the Kinship in Husbandry, which met intermittently throughout the war and was a forerunner of the Soil Association.[41]

Gerard Wallop has been described as 'a seminal influence on the early environmentalist and organic farming movements'.[42] In 1950 he emigrated to Kenya, where he continued to farm, but illness eventually forced him to return to Farleigh Wallop, where he died in 1984. During his absence, the estates were managed by trustees, and farms were again leased. When his successor the 10th earl of Portsmouth assumed

---

36   *Census*, 1851–71.
37   TNA, MAF 68/1895/66; MAF 68/2465/66.
38   Wallop, *Knot of Roots*, 35–6.
39   Conford, 'Organic society', 82–3; 10th earl of Portsmouth, pers. comm., 2016.
40   Above, Farleigh Wallop – Landownership.
41   R. Moore-Colyer and P. Conford, 'A "secret society"? the internal and external relations of the Kinship in Husbandry, 1941–52', *Rural History* 15 (2004), 189–206.
42   *ODNB*, s.v. Wallop, Gerard Vernon, ninth earl of Portsmouth (1898–1984), politician and environmentalist (accessed 25 Nov. 2014).

Figure 37 *Gerard Wallop, 9th earl of Portsmouth, addressing an agricultural meeting on the Farleigh Estate.*

personal control of his Hampshire estates in the 1970s he began to take farms back in hand. In 1987, after the sale of Hatch Warren Farm, he farmed the residual part of the farm south of the M3, and parts of Manor Farm, Farleigh Wallop as well as Manor Farm, Cliddesden. At that time, the estate was known as Farleigh Farms, and the management was shared between Lord Portsmouth and his tenant Bob Fordham, who worked the rest of the estate. Bob Fordham was joined in the tenancy partnership by his son-in-law Chris Allen, who continued to farm under the name Fordham & Allen after Bob Fordham's death in 1984. Lord Portsmouth ceased farming directly in 2007, and since then Fordham & Allen has farmed the entire estate though the extensive woodland on the southern edge of the parish is managed as cover for pheasants, part of the estate economy.[43]

Tenant Farming 1920–2016

The change from sheep farming to cattle, evident at the beginning of the century, continued, and by 1921 there were no sheep in the parish, whilst cattle numbers had

43   10th earl of Portsmouth, pers. comm., 2016.

risen to 180.[44] A report on Home Farm in 1924 described the difficulties encountered by the tenant, Mrs Cole, who farmed 374 a. The farmhouse was described as old, large and rambling; there were four cottages. Water was laid on, but not to the grassland, and the farm was said to be difficult to work owing to the contour and to the very little depth of soil on the higher ground, the chalk coming practically to the surface.[45] In 1941 dairy cattle were the dominant livestock in the parish, a small number of sheep had been reintroduced and pigs were farmed commercially. Arable crops included 390 a. wheat, 181 a. barley, 448 a. oats, 109.5 a. mixed corn and 180 a. potatoes.[46] Hatch Warren Farm was then part of the parish following boundary changes in 1932, so statistics relate to three farms and a much increased acreage. There was a total agricultural workforce of 61 in the parish, possibly including Belgian refugees, followed by Italian and then German prisoners of war who worked on Hatch Warren Farm and maybe elsewhere.[47]

Rex Paterson (1902–78) was a dairy farmer who rented Hatch Warren Farm in 1937 at a time when Hatch was part of Farleigh Wallop parish. An advocate of a cheap, grass-based system of dairy production, he farmed other land in Hampshire as well as farms in Wales, a total at one time of nearly 10,000 a., but Hatch Warren remained the centre of his enterprise. Locally he had six dairy herds, each of 60 cows, increasing to around 80 in the 1980s, with a central dairy at Manor Farm, Farleigh Wallop.[48]

During the Second World War, Paterson, as required by the food production campaign, reduced his area of grassland and converted pasture to the growth of arable crops though not necessarily in the manner desired by the Hampshire War Agricultural Executive Committee (Hants WAEC).[49] A controversial figure at times, he was eventually vindicated in his dispute with the Hants WAEC, in which he claimed victimisation by officials over his cropping plans.[50] His landlord, the 9th earl of Portsmouth, was vice-chairman of the Hants WAEC, which must have led to a problematic relationship between the two men underlined by their very different views on land management and the role of landlords. Paterson returned to dairy farming after the war, becoming one of Britain's largest dairy farmers with 3,750 dairy cows in the early 1970s.[51] His belief that grass and grass silage could make a significant contribution to milk production helped to transform dairy farming; Hatch Warren became a magnet for visitors from Britain and overseas eager to learn about his system of grassland dairy farming.[52] Rex Paterson is remembered for two particular contributions to agriculture: a low-cost, outdoor bail system of milk production – in effect a portable milking parlour – and the Paterson-Tasker buckrake, a tractor-mounted machine designed to revolutionise the process of silage making, manufactured by Taskers of Abbots Ann, Andover. In 1964 Paterson

44   TNA, MAF 68/3026/66.
45   HRO, 15M84/3/1/1/58.
46   TNA, MAF 68/3979/66.
47   John Paterson, pers. comm., 2015.
48   Idem.
49   TNA, MAF 32/977/66: the acreage of arable crops was given as 1,292 a. but the figure was then crossed out; J. Martin, 'Rex Paterson (1903–1978): pioneer of grassland dairy farming and agricultural innovator' in R.W. Hoyle (ed.) *The Farmer in England, 1650–1980* (Farnham, 2013), 295–324.
50   *ODNB*, s.v. Paterson, Rex Munro (1902–1978), agricultural innovator and farmer (accessed 1 Dec. 2015).
51   John Paterson, pers. comm., 2015.
52   R. Paterson, *Milk from Grass* (Massey Ferguson Papers 2, 1965).

was chairman of the Oxford Farming Conference and his services to agriculture were recognised when he was awarded an OBE.[53]

From 1973, John Paterson was the tenant of both Manor Farm and Hatch Warren Farm. Unlike his father who had a number of small herds on several sites, he kept one herd of 300 Friesians, together, at Manor Farm but gave this up having increasingly turned to arable farming. Crops included 50 per cent wheat, 50 per cent barley and a 'pick your own' scheme with 30 a. strawberries, 5 a. raspberries and 25 a. vegetables. This scheme proved popular with people from Basingstoke. In 1973 there had been 13 employees, by 1987 three men were engaged on the arable staff and two on the 'pick your own'.[54]

In 2016 Chris Allen of Fordham & Allen was responsible for all the farm land in Farleigh Wallop, which was divided between arable cultivation and pasture for a closed herd of 200 pedigree Holstein Friesian cows. Some beef cows were also kept. The main crops were milling wheat for bread making, malting barley for whisky and beer, poppies for morphine, oil seed rape and beans.[55]

Crafts, Commerce and Services

Evidence of craft work or other industries is restricted to the 17th century, when Murrogh Jorden (d. 1649) was known to be a brewer, and to the late 19th and early 20th centuries when a clay pit, kiln and brickyard were located beside the pond at Broadmere.[56] There is no evidence for milling but the field names, Upper and Lower Windmill, which were recorded in the north-east of the parish in 1842 indicate the former presence of a windmill.[57] The period during which the mill operated is not known. It would have milled grain for the manor and may have served the whole estate as no mills have been identified in Cliddesden. Both parishes would have been dependent on wind rather than water for milling as there are no suitable watercourses. Farleigh on the higher ground was the better site for a windmill and Upper Windmill field reached a height of 634 ft.[58] An enclosure map dated 1743 shows a windmill in Dummer close to the boundary with Farleigh Wallop and Nutley, which could have been available to Farleigh Wallop farmers.[59]

Commercial enterprises were limited. In 1901 a coal carter and a coal and coke merchant were resident, suggesting a local fuel business.[60] There was a small shop at Broadmere from the 1930s to the 1980s.[61] Portsmouth Estates installed an anaerobic digester on the site of the redundant central dairy in 2014, providing heat and hot water

53   *ODNB*, s.v. Paterson, Rex Munro (1902–1978), agricultural innovator and farmer (accessed 1 Dec 2015).
54   John Paterson, pers. comm., 2015.
55   Chris Allen, pers. comm., 2016.
56   HRO, 15M84/3/1/1/110; *Census*, 1871; OS 1st edn 1:10,560, Hampshire sheet XXVI, 1875 and later edns.
57   HRO, 21M65/F7/87/1–2.
58   HRO, 8M61/82.
59   HRO, 120M79/1.
60   *Census*, 1901.
61   10th earl of Portsmouth, pers. comm., 2016.

for all the estate houses. It consisted of two biomass boilers fuelled by wood chips, and the by-products were spread on the fields – an appropriate continuation of the 9th earl's organic principles.[62] In 2016 Farleigh House was opened as a conference centre and function venue, offering opportunities for a wide range of private and corporate events.[63]

Chalk Pits

Around 30 chalk pits once existed in the parish scattered across the area, contrasting with only four pits in Cliddesden.[64] Chalk burnt into lime was used as a soil improver, the number of pits indicating the poorer quality of the higher land in Farleigh Wallop with its covering of clay with flints.

62   *Basingstoke Gaz.*, 20 Dec. 2014.
63   www.farleighwallop.com/farleighhouse (accessed 10 Apr. 2016).
64   OS 1st edn 1:10,560, Hampshire sheets XVIII, 1877, XXVI, 1875.

A CLOSE RELATIONSHIP HAS EXISTED between the people and communities of Farleigh Wallop and Cliddesden based not only on proximity but as a result of the two manors being in single ownership from 1486, four centuries of a combined ecclesiastical parish, a shared school and several shared charities. The manor house lay in Farleigh Wallop, from 1579 to 1982 the rectory was in Cliddesden and the Board school was built on the boundary between the two parishes. Wills and other records show the intermingling of families and activities, nevertheless Farleigh Wallop maintained its independence, illustrated by the fact that it still had a separate parish meeting in 2016.

Social Structure and Character

In 1086 Farleigh Wallop's population was similar in size to that of Cliddesden but with 15 villeins, seven bordars and only three slaves it had a different social mix, with more higher-status members, and the value of the estate was also higher than that of its neighbour.[1] Village society in 1327, as revealed by lay subsidy assessments of that year, consisted of the lord of the manor Roger de Mortimer, who was unlikely to have been resident, and six tenants who appear to have been from the upper or middling ranks of the peasantry. The rector would have been exempt from this tax, as would those excused payment because of poverty. Assessments varied from 11s., required from the lord of the manor, to sums of between 4s. 6d. from Adam de Houndemulle and 12d., the lowest demand. Amicia de Echyngeham, the only woman mentioned, was assessed to pay 4s., third highest in the list.[2] In 1333 the numbers of those assessed to pay tax had risen to 11 and the total assessment had nearly doubled to 51s.[3]

The Black Death laid its mark upon Farleigh Wallop. A succession of rectors between 1348 and 1350 suggests the impact of plague[4] and the settlement around the church appears to have been deserted at this time or to have declined over the following years. A small hamlet later re-established itself around Farleigh House, some distance to the south.[5]

Farleigh Wallop remained small. Only two householders are mentioned in the lay subsidy rolls of 1586, Sir Henry Wallop at Farleigh House and Robert Kiftell, yeoman.[6] Sir Henry was assessed to pay 13s. 3d. and Kiftell 2s. 8d. Robert Kiftell's family and social

---

1   *Domesday*, 122.
2   *Hants Tax 1327*, 41.
3   TNA, E 179/242/15A, rot. 6.
4   Below, Farleigh Wallop – Religious History.
5   Above, Farleigh Wallop – Introduction.
6   *Hants Subsidy 1586*, 54.

ties lay within a radius of 12–15 miles. He held lands at Northington and Swarraton and the lease of a house at Dummer, as well as his house at Farleigh Wallop. Kiftell, who probably originated from Dummer, asked to be buried there and left 6s. 8d. to Dummer church and 20d. to the poor of Dummer.[7]

Three householders appear in the 1665 hearth tax records; Henry Wallop at Farleigh House with 17 hearths, John Hockley and John Taplyn each with four hearths. Farleigh House stands out as a grand residence and contrasts with the houses of the two yeomen which, nevertheless, would probably have been substantial farm houses of moderately prosperous men.[8] This is supported by probate material of the time. Thomas Taplyn senior (d. 1661), father of John and of seven other children, left £620 amongst them.[9] The inventory of another yeoman, Robert Tilborow (d. 1668), valued his possessions at £357 17s. 9d. and included linen, cushions, plate, drinking glasses and a looking glass, illustrating the development of more comfortable homes in the second half of the 17th century.[10]

The residents of Farleigh House would have had an entirely different lifestyle from the yeomen farmers and the agricultural labourers who made up the rest of this small, compact community. A short series of accounts from the late 16th century during the absence in Ireland of Sir Henry Wallop (I) provides a glimpse of the social life at Farleigh House. The accountants came several times a year to receive the accounts and to take the annual audit. These were social as well as business occasions, and considerable quantities of extra food and wine were bought for them. The house was used freely by Sir Henry's friends and relatives at other times, on one occasion for a six-day celebration of his brother's marriage. Hundreds of gallons of white wine and claret were bought in anticipation of Sir Henry's return in 1584, but as he did not come home, the wine was sold at a discount to two Basingstoke innkeepers and to a good friend and neighbour.[11]

Other evidence of the wealth and possessions of Wallop family members is found in inventories such as that of Sir Oliver Wallop (d. 1566) which describes the 17 main rooms of the house including the great chamber with its expensive hangings, the chapel bedroom and the armoury, its contents reflecting Sir Oliver's life as a soldier and containing two pairs of corselets with their furniture, a demi lance harness and a range of rivets, jacks, curriers and arrows.[12] The will and inventory of Jane Aubrey (d. 1620), aunt of Sir Henry Wallop (I), provides a detailed picture of her wardrobe – silk gowns, petticoats, kirtles, stomachers and 'cuffs of lawn' – as well as the rich furnishings of her bedroom that included a crimson damask and gold tester and curtains, the bed covered by a cloth of crimson and gold satin.[13]

At the end of the 18th century, cottages built at Broadmere, known as Poor Cottages, reveal the presence of less privileged members of the local society.[14] In 1851 there were 106 residents of Farleigh Wallop living in 17 households of whom 60 were male and 46

7   HRO, 1588A/044.
8   Hearth Tax, 218.
9   HRO, 1661A/110.
10   HRO, 1668B/56.
11   HRO, 44M69/E5/1.
12   HRO, 21M65/D2/18.
13   HRO, 1620A/003.
14   HRO, 15M84/3/1/3/31.

female.[15] Housing was limited to employees of the estate in this effectively 'closed' parish. Whilst a high number of residents had been born in the parish or in the surrounding area – 37 and 34 respectively – 14 people had been born outside Hampshire, including two farmers from Lincolnshire and Wiltshire and five servants from Ireland. This suggests that the Wallop family recruited tenants and staff from contacts across the country and from their properties elsewhere.[16]

Farleigh Wallop was not untouched by the agricultural uprising known as the Swing Riots that took place in much of southern England in the latter part of 1830. Difficult economic conditions and a succession of poor harvests fuelled protests that included the destruction of threshing machines – seen as labour-replacing – demands for higher wages and increased poor law allowances. Tenant farmers were caught between paying higher rents imposed by the landlord and responding to the needs of real poverty amongst their workforce. A family of three brothers from the parish were amongst those apprehended in November 1830 having been involved in rioting and demanding money from farmers and landowners in the Basingstoke area. No farms in Farleigh Wallop or Cliddesden were visited by the rioters but nearby Manydown, Down Grange and other properties in Monk Sherborne and Wootton St Lawrence were caught up in the action. The three Keens brothers stood trial before the Special Commission which sat in Winchester in December 1830. John (18) and Richard (34) were transported to Tasmania, Henry (24) escaped conviction. John Keens's conduct record in Tasmania showed his behaviour as unruly but by 1840 he had obtained a free pardon and choosing to remain in Tasmania he married and became the father of ten children – his life probably more prosperous than had he remained in England. He died at the age of 73.[17]

In 1851 Farleigh House had ten resident staff including a butler, coachman, footman and cook. The Routh family were long-term tenants from 1857 until the early 20th century. Mrs Routh and her two daughters, one of whom was a school manager, took an active part in the church and in local life.[18] In 1901 the population of 106 was only slightly lower than in 1851 and the parish differed little from that found a century before – a small, tightly-knit agricultural community engaged on the Farleigh estate.[19]

During the second half of the 20th century, as the need for estate and farm workers diminished with increasing mechanisation, some of the dwellings in Farleigh Wallop were let to private tenants, giving a greater social and occupational mix in the population. The return of the 10th earl of Portsmouth to Farleigh House in 1989 meant that Farleigh Wallop once again had a resident manorial lord and led to his subsequent involvement in the parish, serving as churchwarden of St Andrew's church for 17 years and as chairman of the parish meeting.[20]

15   *Census*, 1851.
16   As well as estates in England, the Wallop family owned Enniscorthy Castle and lands in Ireland from the 16th century to 1914.
17   Chambers, *Rebels*, 56, 249–51.
18   HRO, 15M84/3/1/1/109; *Census*, 1901; HRO, 23A01/A5, 2; below, Farleigh Wallop – Religious History.
19   *Census*, 1851–1901.
20   10th earl of Portsmouth, pers. comm., 2016.

Figure 38 *Farleigh House gardens.*

Social Life

The Life of the Gentry

Two royal visits, those of Elizabeth I in 1591 and Anne of Denmark, wife of James I, in 1603, must count as the highlights of social life at Farleigh House. Elizabeth's visit was short, the 12th and 13th of September; she spent the night before at William Wallop's house at Wield and left to visit the marquis of Winchester at Basing House.[21] Sir Henry Wallop (I) entertained Elizabeth during a six-year interlude from his service in Ireland. William Burghley, lord treasurer, was with the court but was too busy writing letters of state to have 'any jot of leisure to hunt or see hunting occupations for a progress' while at Farleigh House.[22] Burghley did not give any more details, but it is probable that Sir Henry arranged a hunt which the queen could watch from a vantage-point. Sir Henry Wallop (II) was the host of Anne of Denmark. Lady Anne Clifford, who helped to entertain her there, described seeing a comet 'which was a thing observed all over England'.[23]

Sport was part of a way of life for the lords of the manor or their tenants through the ages. Hunting was initially for deer, later for foxes; the sporting potential of north Hampshire recognised in a 1755 advertisement: 'A capital Mansion-House at Farleigh … in a good part of the county for Sporting'.[24] In 1923–4 Captain Roland Orred, tenant of Farleigh House, was master of the Vine Hunt and said to be an 'excellent field master, well mounted and courteous to all'.[25] In the 21st century the Hampshire Hunt met

21   E.K. Chambers, *The Elizabethan Stage*, 4 vols (Oxford, 1923), IV, 106.
22   J. Stevenson (ed.), *Correspondence of Sir Henry Unton* (1847), nos. 42–3.
23   D.J.H. Clifford (ed.), *The Diaries of Lady Anne Clifford* (Stroud, 1992), 26.
24   *St James's Chron.*, May 30–Jun. 1, 1775.
25   J.F.R. Hope, *A History of Hunting in Hampshire* (Winchester, 1950), 53, 86.

Figure 39 *Farleigh Wallop Club House in 2016.*

annually at Farleigh House, in February.[26] Certainly sport has played a significant part in the running of the estate since 1986 when the estate regained woodland that had been leased to the Forestry Commission and re-established the Farleigh Shoot. A further 250 a. of woodland was bought back from the Hackwood Estate in 1999 and in 2013 the shoot was said to be one of Hampshire's finest. [27]

The refurbishment of Farleigh House, completed in 1989, and then the development of the gardens provided an elegant house and grounds as a home for Lord and Lady Portsmouth and for large-scale entertainment including balls and other social and charity events. The gardens have been opened to the public in support of the British Red Cross, Lord Portsmouth being patron of the Hampshire branch of the society, and this occurred on several occasions in 2015.[28] Social life at Farleigh House entered a new phase in 2016 after Lord Lymington converted the house to a conference and function centre.[29]

The Life of the Community

Farleigh Wallop Estate Club was founded in 1934 as a social club for workers from the estate. The thatched premises on The Avenue, opposite Farleigh House, were built in 1985.[30] In 2016 the club was open to members from outside the village, for example from Hatch Warren and other southerly parts of Basingstoke, and alongside a well -stocked bar, held weekly darts nights as well as karaoke and quiz evenings.[31] It extended its hours during the cricket season, a local team playing in the grounds of Farleigh House.[32] Whilst the Farleigh club was the only purpose-built facility for community use in the parish, during the 21st century the barn at Home Farm was used as a venue for carol concerts

26   10th earl of Portsmouth, pers. comm., 2016.
27   Hampshire Country Learning, *Teachers' Handbook* (2013).
28   www.debretts.com/peopleoftoday The Rt Hon the Earl of Portsmouth (accessed 29 Dec. 2015).
29   Above, Farleigh Wallop – Economic History.
30   www.farleighwallopclub.co.uk (accessed 29 Dec. 2015).
31   *Hill and Dale*, Jun. 2013.
32   Above, Cliddesden – Social History.

and local charity events. Basingstoke Choral Society performed there in 2008, 2009 and 2014.[33] Between 2003–15 village activities including a sports day and raft-racing on the lake in Farleigh Park took place and in 2016 a parish party was held to celebrate the Queen's 90th birthday.[34] Residents took an active part in the Cliddesden, Farleigh Wallop and Ellisfield Horticultural Society, and joined other groups who met in Cliddesden – such as the Women's Institute – or travelled into Basingstoke for a wider range of social opportunities.[35]

Education

The school established in Cliddesden in 1656 was for poor children from the two parishes of Cliddesden and Farleigh Wallop.[36] In 1833 a small day and Sunday school existed in Farleigh Wallop which nine boys and girls attended and whose instruction was paid for by Mrs Paxton.[37] The united Board school, which opened in 1876, served the parishes of Cliddesden, Farleigh Wallop and Ellisfield. Known as Cliddesden School, it was actually sited in the parish of Farleigh Wallop, adjoining the boundary with Cliddesden parish.[38] A full account of the school is contained in the chapter on the social history of Cliddesden.[39] The building, extended at various times, was the primary school which children from Farleigh Wallop attended in 2015. Secondary education was provided in Basingstoke.

Numbers of children from Farleigh Wallop attending the old school rose from nine in 1851 to 22 in 1861. The age range of these pupils was 5–12 in 1851 and 4–13 in 1861. Not all children attended school; in 1851 two 11 and 12 year-olds were employed as carter boys, a 10 year-old boy was recorded as an agricultural labourer, an 11 year-old girl was employed as a nurse to two small children and a 12 year-old girl remained at home. Education became compulsory between the ages of five and ten in 1880 and by 1881, after the new school had opened, numbers were 24, amongst them a number of 13 year-olds. By 1901 there were 28 children aged between four and 14 years in the parish.[40] In 2015 only two children were pupils at Cliddesden school.[41]

In 1954 Farleigh House was leased to a private school which was known as Farleigh House School. Temporary buildings were erected in the grounds to provide laboratories, classrooms, a dining hall and gym. When the lease expired in 1983 the school relocated to Redrice, near Andover.[42]

---

33   Information from Basingstoke Choral Society.
34   Below, Farleigh Wallop – Local Government.
35   *Hill and Dale*, Jun. 2013–Dec. 2015.
36   Above, Cliddesden – Social History.
37   *Educ. Enquiry Abstract*, 843.
38   HRO, 15M/84/E6/4/234.
39   Above, Cliddesden – Social History.
40   *Census*, 1851–61, 1881, 1901.
41   Information provided by the school.
42   10th earl of Portsmouth, pers. comm., 2016.

Charities and Welfare

Charity

The Wallop family was an important source of charitable giving. As lords of both
Cliddesden and Farleigh from the 15th century, they were able to manage the charities
of the two parishes together. The full account of these charities is therefore given in the
social history of Cliddesden. Although only occasionally resident after the 1670s, their
interest in the parish remained, in part, from their continued use of Farleigh Wallop
church as a family memorial chapel. The gifts of Ann Doddington and Theodosia
Wallop, daughters of Sir Henry Wallop (I) formed the basis of endowed charities, added
to by Dorothy Wallop née Bluett (d. 1702) and rectors Edward Mooring (d. 1673) and
William Dobson (d. 1731).[43] The bequest of Thomas Fellow of Farleigh Wallop (d.
1738) formed a separate charity for the poor.[44] A Charity Commission scheme of 1899
incorporated all the charities benefitting Farleigh Wallop and Cliddesden.[45] Distribution
of such charities was undertaken on the basis of one third to residents of Farleigh Wallop
and two thirds to residents of Cliddesden.

Poor Relief

Help for the poor came in two forms: charitable giving of individuals and statutory
support of the poor law through the parish rates. Bequests from parishioners included
that of John Lamboll (d. 1605) who left his apparel and the residue of his estate to be
bestowed to such poor people as his executors thought fit [46] and Nathaniel Phipps
(d. 1630) who gave 20s. for the poor.[47] Murrogh Jorden, a brewer (d. 1649) left 30s.
to the poor of Cliddesden and bequests to the poor of Upton Grey, Ellisfield, Preston
Candover and Nutley, as well as to 15 individuals in Farleigh Wallop.[48] Later in the
17th century other residents of Farleigh Wallop left bequests to the poor of Cliddesden,
sums varying from £1 to £5, possibly meaning help to be distributed in both parishes,
combined as an ecclesiastical benefice from 1579.[49] Bequests from rectors made in the
18th and early 19th centuries were specifically directed to be for the benefit of the poor
in both Cliddesden and Farleigh Wallop,[50] as were legacies from John Wallop, viscount
Lymington in 1749 and the 1st earl of Portsmouth in 1762.[51]

---

43   Above, Cliddesden – Social History.
44   Ibid.
45   www.charity-commission.gov.uk. See above, Cliddesden – Social History for details of the scheme and
     subsequent amendments.
46   HRO, 1605A/53.
47   TNA, PROB 11/158/267.
48   HRO, 1649A/36.
49   TNA, PROB 11/198/104; HRO, 1649A/36; 1661A/110.
50   Above, Cliddesden – Social History.
51   Ibid.

Little is known about the use of poor relief in the parish as few overseers' accounts remain.[52] Expenditure varied from £32 17s. 9d. in 1776 to £110 4s.1d. in 1803, more than doubling to £243 10s. 0d. in 1818 – the period after the end of the French wars when the cost of food was particularly high – dropping in 1829 to £87 18s. 0d. but rising again from 1830 to reach £254 1s. 0d. in 1832.[53] This was a time of great poverty for agricultural labourers, reflected in the high payments of relief.

Poor cottages existed at Broadmere in the 1760s–70s, the rent of £1 10s. a year presumably paid by the overseers to the earl of Portsmouth.[54] In 1818, a scheme whereby farmers in the parish provided every cottager with a portion of land on which to grow potatoes was both a benevolent response to the conditions of the time and a way of diminishing the pressure on the poor rates. Seed potatoes were supplied by the rector, David Davies, and the produce was considered to be equal to the yearly consumption of each family.[55]

In 1834 the Poor Law Amendment Act introduced poor law unions and Farleigh Wallop became part of the Basingstoke Union, responsibility for the poor passing to the Union guardians based at the workhouse in Old Basing. Expenditure fell dramatically, with Farleigh Wallop contributing only £36 to the Union in 1837 and a mere £27 4s. 0d. the following year, an example of the efficacy of the government's cost-cutting legislation.[56] By the end of the century, in 1897–8, this had risen to £52.[57]

Settlement and Bastardy

There appears to have been little movement in or out of this small parish and such that there was seems to have been very local. In 1716 a settlement certificate was issued for William Barker and his wife who had moved to Basing.[58] Jane Goodall a single woman, when pregnant in 1769, named Richard Hall – late servant of farmer Stephen Lawes of Cliddesden – as the father and declared the child likely to be born a bastard and chargeable to the parish of Farleigh Wallop.[59] In 1773 the same Jane, still a single woman, attempted to enter Cliddesden three times, once in the company of four men. She was removed on all three occasions.[60] One removal order into the parish from Preston Candover, in 1795, also related to a pregnant single woman,[61] whilst Thomas Bennett, his wife and two children were removed from Old Basing to Farleigh Wallop in 1831.[62] William Keynes, a labourer, was held in the Odiham bridewell for three weeks in November 1801 charged with 'departing and leaving his family as a charge to the parish'.[63]

52   HRO, 68M72/DU22–3. The only accessible accounts (1888–1927) are for total income and expenditure.
53   *Poor Abstract, 1777*, 453; *Poor Abstract, 1804*, 450; *Poor Rate Rtns*, (1822), 154; (1835), 173.
54   HRO, 15M84/3/1/3/31.
55   *Jackson's Oxford Jnl*, 1 May 1819.
56   *Poor Rate Rtns*, (1837, ii), 168; (1838, ii), 16.
57   HRO, 15M84/7/4/4.
58   HRO, 3M70/52/9.
59   HRO, 44M69/G3/385.
60   HRO, 44M69/G3/454; 44M69/G3/440.
61   HRO, 44M69/G3/774.
62   HRO, 3M70/55/78.
63   HRO, 44M69/G3/873.

Medical Services

Parishioners were dependent on medical services in Basingstoke, if financially able to access them. In the 19th century this included a number of doctors and surgeons as well as the Cottage Hospital (opened in 1879). The longer established County Hospital in Winchester was also available for those who could reach it. In the late 1930s a Dr Hunt lived in Farleigh Wallop and provided some medical services in the Farleigh Wallop club house.[64]

64   BTH, Irene Holloway (BAHS 124).

LOCAL GOVERNMENT

Manorial and Hundred Courts

THERE IS NO DIRECT EVIDENCE for manorial courts at Farleigh Wallop, although occasional references in the 16th-century accounts of Sir Henry Wallop's bailiffs indicate that courts then took place informally in the presence of a bailiff.[1] The tenants of the manor owed suit to the hundred court of Bermondspit, which was held at Nutley, two miles to the south, and to the sheriff's tourn there.[2] The bailiff attended and paid their contributions to the national tax called 'fifteenths' out of Sir Henry Wallop's own money in 1587–8.[3] No other manorial records for Farleigh Wallop have survived.

Parish Government and Officers

Farleigh Wallop had its own parish officers until it was joined with Cliddesden as a united benefice in 1579. The parish registers were combined at this time but the parish continued with its own churchwardens and overseers of the poor, for example, Henry Dalman, churchwarden in Farleigh Wallop in 1702.[4] Normally, parishes had two churchwardens and two overseers but in 1716, a settlement certificate signed by John Hooker, churchwarden, and John Kersley, overseer of the poor, contained the comment 'there being but one churchwarden and one overseer'.[5] Sadly, no churchwardens' accounts and only the overseers' accounts for the period 1888–1927 survive.[6] Henry Paxton was the first guardian elected as Farleigh Wallop's board member on the Basingstoke Union, which was established as a result of the 1834 Poor Law Amendment Act and which assumed responsibility for poor relief. The first meeting of the Union was in 1835; the 37 parishes which formed the Union were each represented by one member.[7]

The Local Government Act of 1894 made provision for parishes with a population of less than 300 to hold a parish meeting rather than establish a parish council. Farleigh Wallop was one such parish and the situation did not alter when, in 1932, Hatch was transferred to it, the combined population only reaching 132. The rector, John Seymour Allen, was the first chairman, followed in 1896 by John Morris. An estimate for the rate

1   Above, Cliddesden – Local Government.
2   *VCH Hants* III, 355–6.
3   HRO, 44M69/E5/2.
4   HRO, Q25/2/13/4.
5   HRO, 3M70/52/9. Cliddesden claimed to have only one overseer in 1773: HRO, 44M69/G3/454.
6   HRO, 68M72/DU22–3; above, Farleigh Wallop – Social History.
7   HRO, PL3/5/1.

in 1898 showed a requirement for the parish to contribute £40 to the Union for relief of the poor, £10 to the school board and £15 to the rural district council for highways. £4 0s.10d. was allocated for use within the parish.[8]

Until 1974 Farleigh Wallop was part of the Basingstoke rural district. In that year it was amalgamated with the borough when Basingstoke and Deane Borough Council was established. The development of Hatch for housing and the subsequent boundary adjustments affected Farleigh Wallop, although it retained its identity as a civil parish.[9] In 2016 the 10th earl of Portsmouth was chairman of the parish meeting, having undertaken this role since about 1989. The main business of the meeting was to discuss Basingstoke matters which might affect Farleigh Wallop. No rate was raised for the parish but a small grant was received each year from the borough council and this was used to support village events.[10]

8   HRO, 15M84/7/4/5.
9   Above, Farleigh Wallop – Introduction.
10   10th earl of Portsmouth, pers. com., 2016; above, Farleigh Wallop – Social History.

RELIGIOUS HISTORY

THE RELIGIOUS HISTORY OF FARLEIGH Wallop has been closely linked with that of Cliddesden and in the mid 16th century the parish became part of a benefice known as Cliddesden cum Farleigh. Nonconformity was virtually non-existent until the early part of the 20th century, when there was a short-lived Congregational chapel.

Parochial Organisation

The small, stone and flint cruciform church of St Andrew stands isolated in a field some distance from the hamlet of Farleigh Wallop. It is of 18th and 19th century origin though built on the site of a medieval church and was known to have had its own rector from before 1277.[1] The dedication to St Andrew was first noted in 1814 although an alternative dedication to St John has occasionally been cited, without supporting evidence.[2] In 1579 the church was annexed to Cliddesden,[3] a union that lasted for nearly four centuries until they were separated in 1954. Farleigh Wallop was then joined with Ellisfield, a neighbouring parish to the south-east, to form a new benefice.[4] This was dissolved in 1972 to create the benefice of Ellisfield with Farleigh Wallop and Dummer, a parish to the west, [5] and in 1983 a benefice was formed consisting of Cliddesden, Farleigh Wallop, Ellisfield and Dummer, sharing one priest and with a rectory at Ellisfield.[6] This became a single parish in 2008, known as Farleigh,[7] and in 2010 formed part of a new, united benefice of Farleigh, Candover and Wield with a rector and an associate rector, the latter holding primary pastoral responsibility for the northern parishes including Farleigh Wallop.[8]

1   HRO, 44M69/C7.
2   Bingley, *Hampshire*; *VCH Hants* III, 365; Watney, *Wallop Family* I, xxii. A possible confusion with St John's church at Farley Chamberlayne may have occurred.
3   *Parson and Parish*, 39.
4   HRO, 67M72/PR5, copy of Order in Council pasted into register.
5   HRO, 45M84/4.
6   HRO, 21M65/Orders in Council/Cliddesden.
7   www.allsaintschurchdummer.hampshire.org.uk: parish of Farleigh (accessed 1 Aug. 2013).
8   Winchester Diocesan Office: pastoral scheme, Jul. 2010.

Figure 40 *The church of St Andrew standing isolated in a field.*

Advowson

As in Cliddesden, the advowson followed the descent of the manor.[9] In 1273 a dispute arose over the advowson of Farleigh church when Robert and Joyce de Mortimer claimed it from Henry of Farleigh[10] and in 1275 brought a similar case against the bishop of Winchester on the grounds that he had not admitted a suitable parson to the church of Farleigh although they had recovered the advowson in the royal court.[11] They finally gained it, together with the manor, in 1279.[12] Roger de Mortimer presented in 1334[13] and was succeeded by Robert de la Zouche who presented from 1348,[14] the time of the Black Death, through until – at least – 1367.[15] In the 15th century Sir Nicholas de Valognes and then William Vachell held the manor and presented in 1411 and 1448 respectively.[16] Joint ownership of the land meant that from the mid 15th century the advowson mirrored that of Cliddesden. The first of the Wallop family to present was John Wallop (I) in 1479,[17] followed by his widow, Joan, in 1489.[18] In 1954, when Farleigh Wallop was joined with Ellisfield, alternate turns gave the earl of Portsmouth the right of presentation,[19] followed, in 1960, by Ivy Botry Cannon.[20] In 1972 with the creation of a new benefice of Ellisfield with Farleigh Wallop and Dummer the advowson was vested in the Winchester Diocesan Board of Patronage.[21] The advowson for the benefice of Cliddesden, Farleigh Wallop,

9   Above, Farleigh Wallop – Landownership.
10   TNA, CP 40/3, rot. 36.
11   TNA, CP 40/7, rot. 27d; CP 40/9, rot. 19d.
12   *Placit. in Domo Capit. Abbrev.,* 199.
13   Reg. Orleton II, f. 43.
14   *Reg. Edington* I, 45.
15   *Reg. Edington* I, 202.
16   Reg. Beaufort, f. 88; Reg. Waynflete I, f. 6.
17   Reg. Waynflete I, f. 85v.
18   Lipkin, *Institutions.*
19   HRO, 21M65/A2/14, 81.
20   HRO, 21M65/A2/15, 168.
21   HRO, 45M84/4.

Ellisfield and Dummer, created in 1983, was held jointly by the earl of Portsmouth and the Diocesan Board of Patronage.[22] Presentation arrangements established for the new benefice in 2010 gave alternate patronage of either the Lord Chancellor or the bishop of Winchester, the appropriate diocesan body, the earl of Portsmouth and Sir John Baring, acting together.[23]

Glebe, Tithes and Rectory House

The income of the living arose from glebe and tithes, the rector owning all the tithes in the parish. The church was assessed at £8 0s. 0d. in 1291[24] but by 1341, amidst difficult agricultural conditions, the value had diminished. The endowment of one messuage, a garden and one carucate of land was said to be worth 42s. annually; the tithe of cider, mill, hay and other small tithes with the offerings and mortuary payments amounted to 61s. 9d.[25] In 1535 the value of the living was assessed at £10 12s. 1d.[26] At all three dates the value of Farleigh was higher than that of Cliddesden although in 1535 the difference was only slight. By the time of the tithe award in 1842 the situation had reversed with the tithes of Farleigh Wallop commuted to the sum of £340, paid annually, with a rent of £2 10s. 0d. for glebe land of 9 a. This compared with a commutation of £550 in Cliddesden. Combined, the living of Cliddesden cum Farleigh was a wealthy one.[27] The glebe land consisted of the field to the west of the church and east of Broadmere.[28] It was sold in 1913 to Newton Wallop, 6th earl of Portsmouth for £225.[29] The rectory was annexed to Cliddesden in 1579 with the rectory at Cliddesden used as the parsonage house. No longer needed, the house at Farleigh Wallop was initially let with the rent of 5s. a quarter paid to Robert Richardson, the first rector of both parishes.[30] Its site is not known.

Pastoral Care and Religious Life

The Middle Ages

The first mention of a rector of Farleigh is in 1277 with a reference to 'Henry, once rector of Farleigh ... held tenement lands in Herriard'.[31] William de Marke is shown as serving the parish from 1334 to 1348. Between 1348 and 1350 four rectors followed each other in quick succession.[32] Thomas de Bokenhull succeeded William de Marke in February

---

22 HRO, 21M65/Orders in Council/Cliddesden.
23 Winchester Diocesan Office: pastoral scheme, Jul. 2010.
24 *Tax. Eccl.*, 212.
25 *Nonarum Inquisitiones*, 122.
26 *Valor Eccl.* II, 14.
27 Above, Cliddesden – Religious History.
28 HRO, 21M65/F7/87/1–2, field 109.
29 HRO, 15M84/2/1/8/1.
30 HRO, 44M69/E5/7.
31 HRO, 44M69/C7.
32 Reg. Orleton II, f. 43; *Reg. Edington* I, 45.

1348 in exchange for Eastnor (Herefs.) a benefice in the gift of the bishop of Hereford.[33] Bokenhull's career appears to have progressed swiftly in that he was presented by the bishop of Winchester to the church of Bleadon (Som.), within a month and he was at the papal curia in Avignon when he died in August 1349.[34] In April 1349 Richard of Dorset was instituted to Farleigh [35] and in August of that year William Elyot followed him as rector.[36] The cause of this vacancy was not recorded but death was so common at the time of the Black Death that it was frequently omitted.[37] Elyot, who had served as rector of Cliddesden from March to August 1349, was admonished by Bishop Edington in 1350:

> William Elyot, rector of Farleigh [Wallop], near Basingstoke, neglects the cure of souls and is absent without permission in unknown parts, spending the revenue of the church. They are to admonish him, to get his friends to make him return within a month to resume his ministry and repair the buildings. They are to ensure that the divine service is maintained by some suitable chaplain, supported from the revenue of the church. To report before the Translation of St Thomas the Martyr (7 July). Southwark, 10 June 1350.[38]

Elyot resigned and in November 1350 Thomas le Halterwrighte, who had also been rector of Cliddesden from September 1349, was instituted rector.[39] There followed a slightly more settled period, although Richard Pante only served for one month in 1361[40] and Richard Harries, rector from 1367–72 was cited for non-residence in 1371.[41] Another Pante, William, was rector from 1372-4.[42] John Cambrey was admitted in 1374[43] but a William Pant was the incumbent in 1390 – possibly the same William.[44] In 1398 Sir Nicholas de Valognes obtained a licence for a private chapel in Farleigh House.[45] It is not known who served this chapel but a gap occurs in the records of rectors until Thomas Beworth whose time as rector ended in 1448.[46] Lack of a rector may have been the reason for the request for a private chapel. From then on the parish appears to have been well served by a succession of priests, of whom the first recorded as holding a university degree was William Danby MA Oxon, instituted in 1495.[47] Danby had previously served

33   *Reg. Edington* I, 45; J. Cooper, *Eastnor* (2013), 70.
34   W.H. Bliss (ed.), *Petitions to the Pope, 1342–1419* (1896), 170.
35   *Reg. Edington* I, 79.
36   *Reg. Edington* I, 100.
37   *Reg. Edington* I, xii.
38   *Reg. Edington* II, 32.
39   *Reg. Edington* I, 119.
40   *Reg. Edington* I, 197, 202.
41   *Reg. Wykeham* II, 145.
42   *Reg. Wykeham* I, 43.
43   *Reg. Wykeham* I, 273.
44   TNA, CP 25/1/207/28.
45   *Reg. Wykeham* II, 482; above, Farleigh Wallop – Landownership.
46   Reg. Waynflete, f. 6.
47   Lipkin, *Institutions.*

in the Carlisle diocese.[48] David Griffith was instituted in 1555 and remained for 20 years[49] but by 1575–8 the living was vacant.[50]

A gift for lights and other ornaments in the church made in the early years of the 16th century by the widow of Richard Wallop is evidence of pre-Reformation practices.[51] The 1535 will of Sir Robert Wallop conforms to the religious beliefs of the time. He commended his soul to 'our Lord Jesus Christ, our Lady Saint Mary and to all the saints of Heaven' asking for his body to be buried in the chancel of the parish church at Farleigh, next to his father's tomb. He left 20s. to the mother church at Winchester and to the priory church of Twyneham – he was a brother of the chapter house in both churches – and a further 20s. to the priory church of Southwick. Other gifts included 3s. 4d. to every parish church within four miles of Farleigh, 100 ewes to Farleigh church and 50 ewes to Cliddesden church.[52] By the reign of Elizabeth the will of Sir Oliver Wallop (d. 1566) reveals the ascendance of Protestantism; he bequeathed his soul to 'Almighty God my only maker, redeemer and saviour in whom is my only trust'. He left £3 to the parish church of Farleigh and 40s.to the church of Cliddesden.[53]

1579–1954

In 1579 Farleigh Wallop was joined with Cliddesden to form one benefice with the rectory at Cliddesden and thereafter rectors were inducted to both rectories.[54] An account of rectors from 1579–1954 is contained in the chapter on Cliddesden religious history. Baptism, marriage and burial registers were included with those of Cliddesden until 1839.[55] A register of 'burials in woollen', according to the acts of 1677 and 1678 which were designed to help the wool trade, shows eight members of the Wallop family buried at Farleigh Wallop choosing to be buried in linen and a fine of £10 levied on each occasion.[56]

How far the religious and political upheavals of the 17th century which revealed themselves in the parish with the deprivation of one rector (1636) the ejection (1655) and restoration (1660) of another and the imposition of a Puritan minister during the Interregnum affected the lives and religious beliefs of parishioners may be glimpsed in testamentary evidence.[57] Four wills dating from 1621–61 span this period and each contains a strong declaration of the testators' belief in salvation through the merits of Jesus Christ and of their hopes for everlasting life; that of Murrogh Jorden (d. 1649) a brewer, contains an assurance of his soul's place in eternal glory and his belief that on

48   A.B. Emden, *A Biographical Register of the University of Oxford to A.D. 1500*, 3 vols (Oxford, 1957–9), I, 540. His patron (Joanna Wallop, widow) makes it clear that this was Farleigh Wallop and not Farley Chamberlayne to which Emden linked him.
49   Reg. Horne I, f. 69v; HRO, 21M65/B1/8, 10–12.
50   HRO, 21M65/B1/14.
51   Bingley, *Hampshire*.
52   TNA, PROB 11/25/347.
53   HRO, 21M65/D2/18.
54   *Parson and Parish*, 39; above, Cliddesden – Religious History, for this period.
55   HRO, 31M82/PR1.
56   HRO, 31M82/PR2.
57   Above, Cliddesden – Religious History.

the day of general resurrection he would appear before the judgement seat of Christ.[58] Similar themes are found in the 1738 will of Thomas Fellow who hoped to inherit eternal life amongst those who are 'sanctified and saved'.

As in Cliddesden, no Dissent was said to exist in the parish in 1676, nor in 1788.[59] The influence of the lord of the manor would have had a strong bearing on religious practice in this small, dependent community. The role of the Wallop family in rebuilding, restoring and maintaining the church was, and remains, key to its survival. It has the character of a mortuary chapel in its use for burials of family members, who may or may not have lived at Farleigh Wallop, and the majority of the memorials on the floor and walls are to the family.

In 1810 the church was referred to as a 'chapel of Cliddesden'.[60] Nevertheless, it provided baptism, marriage and burial services for the small population and in 1827 held a service with a sermon each Sunday.[61] Seven people were confirmed in 1832 and two in 1835.[62] In 1851, with a population of 112, average attendance figures were 20 in the morning and 50 in the afternoon.[63] Archdeacon Fearon visiting the church in 1915 commented on the lack of a path to the church, and queried whether there was anyone to come, Farleigh House being empty at the time.[64] In 1936 the bishop of Winchester informed Gerard Wallop, viscount Lymington that it would be 'contrary to Church Order' for him to receive communion or read lessons in Farleigh Wallop church because of his divorce. The bishop acknowledged the interest that Lord Lymington had shown in the church and was sorry for this position.[65] During restoration work to the tower in 1938 the rector, Arthur Badger, held a service every Sunday in the Farleigh Wallop Club.[66]

1954–2016

Edward Quick was the first rector of the new benefice of Ellisfield and Farleigh Wallop[67] followed, in 1960, by the Venerable Richard Rudgard OBE, at one time archdeacon of Basingstoke and chaplain to the Queen.[68] Thomas Kime, rector from 1974, became rector of the new benefice of Cliddesden, Ellisfield, Farleigh Wallop and Dummer in 1983.[69] Services were spread throughout the churches. In 2010 services at Farleigh Wallop were recorded thus:

> A communion service for the Single Parish [is held] at St. Andrew's, Farleigh
> Wallop whenever there is a fifth Sunday in the month. By request, Evensong

58   HRO, 1621A/24; 1626B/028; 1649A/36; 1661A/110.
59   *Compton Census*, 83; *Parson and Parish*, 267.
60   *Doing the Duty*, 30.
61   HRO, 21M65/B5/2, 36.
62   Ibid.
63   *Rel. Census*, 185.
64   HRO, 110M98/1.
65   HRO, 15M84/F249.
66   HRO, 67M72/PR5, appeal pasted into register.
67   *Crockford Clerical Dir.*, 1977–9, 823.
68   Ibid., 883–4.
69   HRO, 21M65/Orders in Council/Cliddesden.

has been celebrated on an occasional basis ... and St Andrew's hosts a candlelit service at 4pm on Christmas Eve, which has proved immensely popular throughout the parish.[70]

Nonconformity

Farleigh Wallop appears to have had no Dissent until the start of the 20th century. The Congregational cause at Farleigh Wallop was established in 1900 under the auspices of the London Street Congregational church, Basingstoke. Initially, services took the form of cottage meetings before, in 1906, a purpose-built chapel was constructed. It was opened on 6th September by Miss Sarah Jane Wallis the mayoress of Basingstoke, who had donated half the cost. Alfred Capes Tarbolton, the minister of the parent church presided at a public meeting later in the day.[71] This chapel was one of seven chapels overseen by an evangelist attached to Basingstoke's London Street Congregational church in the early years of the 20th century.

The chapel was located at Foxhall, some distance from the main settlement on a site owned by the earl of Portsmouth who offered it on a 999-year lease at a nominal rent. The simple building was of corrugated iron with a matchboard interior and could accommodate nearly a hundred people.[72] During the first few years after it was opened, services were held every Sunday evening and in the afternoon there was a Sunday school; there was also a fortnightly Mothers' Meeting.[73] After a promising start, however, it was not long before the cause was struggling. As in many rural chapels the removal of families who had played a crucial role in its activities created difficulties and resulted in the closure of the Sunday school.[74] The chapel was temporarily closed from 1918 to 1920.[75] It reopened in 1921 and hosted well-attended harvest thanksgiving services during the first half of the 1920s. The roof was repaired and a stove installed.[76] However, in 1927 the London Street deacons decided to abandon the work at Farleigh Wallop and the chapel was closed permanently, just over 20 years after it had been opened.[77] It is not clear what happened to the building, but in 2014 there was no sign that a chapel ever existed on the site.

The Church of St Andrew

The church stands on the site of a medieval church which by 1733 was said to have been in a ruinous state and was rebuilt by John Wallop (III), later 1st earl of Portsmouth, who

70 www.allsaintschurchdummer.hampshire.org.uk: parish of Farleigh (accessed 1 Aug. 2013).
71 *Hants and Berks. Gaz.*, 8 Sept. 1906.
72 London Street Congregational church: deacons' meetings minutes, Mar. 1905; *Hants and Berks. Gaz.*, 8 Sept. 1906.
73 *Basingstoke Congregational Magazine*, 3, n.s. no. 3, Mar. 1910.
74 *Basingstoke and District Congregational Magazine*, 5, n.s. no. 1, Jan. 1912.
75 HRO, 127M94/62/62–4.
76 London Street Congregational church: deacons' meetings minutes, 1924–5.
77 Ibid., 6 May 1927.

Figure 41 *The church of St Andrew: pen and ink drawing, n.d. but before 1840, showing the classical former west front of the 1733 rebuilding, with the earl of Portsmouth's achievement.*

may have been his own architect.[78] A late 15th or 16th century chest tomb on the south side of the chancel survives from the first church. The inscriptions on it are worn away but a shield bears the Wallop coat of arms.[79] A pen and ink drawing of the church as it appeared after 1733 shows the mixture of perpendicular and classical styles with the classical west front bearing the earl of Portsmouth's achievement. It has been described as a rare example of early Georgian gothic.[80] Restoration took place in 1871–2 when the classical former west front was destroyed and the west tower added.[81]

The grade II* listed church is built in a cruciform shape, a symmetrical cross of five squares; the outer walls are flint with the corners having quoins on each face, strengthened by brick pilasters, and the roof is tiled. There is one window on each outside wall, except the south side of the southern arm. Six of the stone windows have three lights with cusped heads within a rectangular frame and are probably from the original design in 1733 whilst four, including the east window and northern arm, have

78   Bingley, *Hampshire*.
79   Pevsner, *North Hampshire*, 268; NHLE, no. 1302322 'Ch. of St Andrew' (accessed 9 Nov. 2016).
80   Pevsner, *North Hampshire*, 268.
81   Bingley, *Hampshire*; Pevsner, *North Hampshire*, 268.

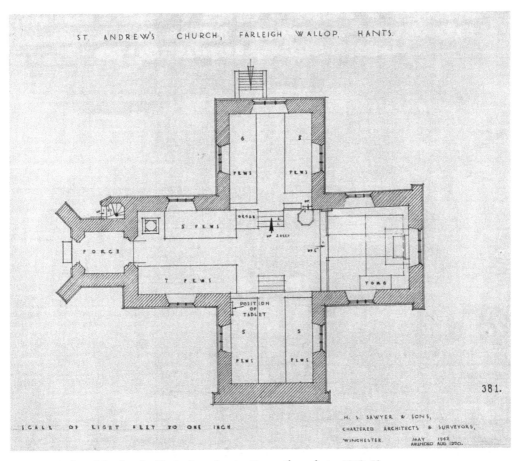

Figure 42 *A plan of the church of St Andrew showing its cruciform shape, 1948–50.*

painted hoods, hood moulds and tracery and are from the restoration in 1871.[82] The flint tower with stone dressings is of perpendicular style, with a crenellated parapet and openings at the bell-stage under a traceried head. Entry to the church is through the porch at the base of the tower.

Inside, the north and south arms of the church have raised floors approached by central flights of steps. There is a screened area for a vestry on the north side.[83] The eastern arm has early 18th-century altar rails with twisted balusters and carved heraldic wild goats or chamois as finials, made for the staircase at Hurstbourne Park and brought here in 1938.[84] The elaborate reredos and cill-height linenfold panelling was installed in 1913 in memory of Mrs Routh, tenant of Farleigh House, with her husband, Col. Routh, from 1857.[85] Above are painted panels with the Ten Commandments and the Lord's Prayer. The pulpit, lectern and font are Victorian. The timber-framed roof is arch-braced,

82 NHLE, no. 1302322 'Ch. of St Andrew' (accessed 9 Nov. 2016).
83 HRO, 21M65/148F/10. The vestry was created in 1962.
84 HRO, 21M65/148F/2.
85 HRO, 110M98/1. The Routh family were tenants of Farleigh House from 1857 for about 50 years and were benefactors of the church and much involved in parish life; above, Farleigh Wallop-Social History.

Figure 43 *The interior of the church of St Andrew showing the chancel.*

with two bays in each arm. There are three bells by Mears and Stainbank which were given to the church by Eliza Routh, F. A. Routh and A. S. Routh in 1872.[86] The tenor bell was re-cast in 1963.[87] Plate consists of a silver chalice and paten cover, 1568, and a silver paten *c.*1680 bearing the quartered arms of Wallop and Borlase surrounded by a plumed ornament. There is also a silver flagon with the inscription: 'The gift of John Wallop Esq. to the Parish Church of Farly Wallop in the County of Southampton Anno 1692' and the arms of Wallop within a scrolled and festooned oval shield.[88] An oak plaque on the wall close to the pulpit is a memorial to three men who died in the two World Wars and was designed and given in 1958 by Edgar Oates, churchwarden and himself a veteran.[89]

The church, described as 'originally a Wallop chapel', has many Wallop memorials.[90] There are five 18th-century armorial ledger stones commemorating members of the family in the chancel floor. An 1829 diocesan register records: 'South chancel or aisle of Farleigh church belongs to Ld Portsmouth whose family vaults are [t]here. In vault

86   W.E. Colchester, *Hampshire Church Bells* (Winchester, 1920), 80.
87   HRO, 21M65/148F/11.
88   Braithwaite, *Church Plate*, 99–100.
89   HRO, 21M65/148F/10.
90   HRO, 110M98/1.

Figures 44 and 45 Left, Wallop family memorials in the south arm of the church and right, carved wooden chamois with metal pennant, one of two finials on the altar rail.

under N transept are 19 coffins, a skeleton'.[91] In the southern arm are several Wallop inscriptions including two large, twin tablets with pilasters and pediments dedicated to the 1st earl of Portsmouth, who died in 1762, and his wife and daughter who had predeceased him. Between them lies a smaller memorial to the 2nd earl and his wife Urania, showing a seated woman by an urn and weeping willow. Above the door, on the west wall, a Grinling Gibbons-style garland of wood has been used as a surround to a plain wooden tablet to the 8th earl.

The 20th century opened with the church said by Archdeacon Fearon to be 'in poor condition' with much damp around the chancel, no gutter and earth around the walls. By 1915 the situation had improved but in 1938 the fabric was in poor condition again and the rector, Arthur Badger, appealed for financial help:

> It [St Andrew's] stands like a flint stone cross, recumbent upon the grass, hidden away in green meadows, a silent witness for Christ through the centuries in this quiet English countryside … alas the mortar perished, and damp and weather added their part to neglect, until gable walls bulged, window mullions became out of truth and dry rot and death watch beetle did their work of destruction.

91 HRO, 21M65/B5/2.

The tower became unsafe, one of the buttresses no longer acted as a support, and masses of masonry fell to the ground.[92]

Repairs were undertaken and a tablet records that the walls of the church were restored in memory of Beatrice, countess of Portsmouth (d. 1935).[93] In 1948–9 electric light and heating were installed at an estimated cost of £380, met by the earl of Portsmouth and parishioners.[94] In 1959 the roof was stripped and wood sprayed to eradicate beetle trouble, the walls of the south transept were given a waterproof seal and floorboards in the transept were renewed, the work amounting to £1,000.

Further restoration including internal decoration was carried out in 1980 in memory of Ruth, Lady Lymington, the costs of £5,000 defrayed by her son Quentin Wallop, later 10th earl of Portsmouth. A plaque on the south wall near to the west door bearing a mermaid from the family crest records the work. The diocesan authorities were worried that the mermaid was 'not exactly a Christian symbol' but agreed its inclusion, noting that a number of mermaids already existed in the church.[95]

In 2017 the well-maintained church with white painted interior walls and light oak seating had an airy and attractive appearance.

92   HRO, 67M72/PR5, appeal pasted into register.
93   HRO, 21M65/148F/3.
94   HRO, 21M65/148F/6.
95   HRO, 21M65/F1981/16.

The area described in this volume has, in the first quarter of the 21st century, come to look toward Basingstoke without being dominated by it. While Hatch has been absorbed into the growing town, the M3 motorway has provided a substantial physical barrier which has contributed to maintaining the rural character of Farleigh Wallop, and to a lesser extent, Cliddesden.

In September 2017, an application to build 40 houses on Southlea Meadow, Farleigh Road, in Cliddesden was rejected by Basingstoke and Deane Borough Council planning committee.[1] This development was deemed to be beyond the bounds of the existing developed area of the village, already expanded by housing occupied by commuters either to Basingstoke or from Basingstoke to London, Southampton or Salisbury. In 2018 an appeal was lodged against the planning decision.

Whilst Farleigh Wallop has not experienced any such similar growth, the changing role of Farleigh House from 2016 may have consequences for the social and economic life of the parish. Proposals and developments such as these are indicative of the pressures faced by these parishes in their struggle to maintain their own identity in the 21st century. The M3 has so far restricted the southwards expansion of Basingstoke but maintaining the separation is a continuing concern to both communities.

In spring 2018 the pedigree Holstein Friesian herd was disbanded. The decision was influenced by recent regulations requiring large investments to bring old dairy buildings up to new standards, coupled with uncertainty about the future of dairy farming.

---

1   Basingstoke and Deane Borough Co. 16/04690/FUL: http://pad.basingstoke.gov.uk/
    documents/4753/01/14/05/01140598.PDF; https://www.cliddesdenparishcouncil.info/southlea-
    meadow/ (accessed 24 Oct. 2017).

a.	acre(s)
Alumni Cantab.	J.A. Venn (ed.), *Alumni Cantabrigienses 1752–1900* (6 vols, Cambridge, 1940–54)
Alumni Oxon.	J. Foster (ed.), *Alumni Oxonienses 1500–1714* (4 vols, Oxford, 1891–2); *1715–1886* (4 vols, Oxford, 1887–8)
Attwood, *Struggle*	A. Attwood, 'The struggle for a Methodist meeting', *Basingstoke Gazette*, 15 Dec. 1978
BDBC	Basingstoke and Deane Borough Council
BHAS	Basingstoke Historical and Archaeological Society
BTH	Basingstoke Talking History
Baigent and Millard, *Basingstoke*	F.J. Baigent and J.E. Millard, *A History of the Ancient Town and Manor of Basingstoke in the County of Southampton*, 2 vols (Basingstoke, 1889)
Banham and Faith, *Anglo-Saxon Farms*	D. Banham and R. Faith, *Anglo-Saxon Farms and Farming* (Oxford, 2014)
Berry, *Hants. Gen.*	W. Berry, *Genealogies: Pedigrees of the Families in the County of Hants* (1833)
Bingley, *Hampshire*	HRO, 16M79/15: William Bingley, *History of Hampshire, Parishes, C*
Bowie, 'Farming practices'	G. Bowie, 'Re-defining farming practices on the Hampshire and Wiltshire chalklands, 1250–1850', *Proc. Hants F.C.* 70 (2015), 136–54
Braithwaite, *Church Plate*	P.R.P. Braithwaite, *Church Plate of Hampshire* (1909)
Cal. Close	*Calendar of the Close Rolls preserved in the Public Record Office* (HMSO, 1892–1963)
Cal. Inq. p.m.	*Calendar of Inquisitions post mortem preserved in the Public Record Office* (HMSO, 1904–2009)
Cal. Inq. p.m. Hen. VII	*Calendar of Inquisitions post mortem, Henry VII* (HMSO, 1898–1955)

Cal. SP Dom.   *Calendar of State Papers, Domestic Series*
                                        (HMSO, 1856–2006)

Cal. Pat.   *Calendar of the Patent Rolls preserved in
                                        the Public Record Office* (HMSO, 1891–1986)

Cat. Anct. Deeds   *A Descriptive Catalogue of Ancient Deeds in
                                        the Public Record Office* (HMSO, 1890–1915)

Chambers, *Rebels*   J. Chambers, *Rebels of the Fields: Robert Mason
                                        and the Convicts of the Eleanor* (Letchworth,
                                        *c.*1995)

Charities Report   *Commissioners of Inquiry into Charities in
                                        England and Wales: 14th Report* (Parl. Papers
                                        1826 (382))

Clidd. log summary   Cliddesden School, summary of log held by
                                        school

Coates, *Place-names*   R. Coates, *The Place-names of Hampshire*
                                        (1989)

Complete Peerage   G.E. Cokayne, *The Complete Peerage* (1887–98)

Compton Census   A. Whiteman (ed.), *The Compton Census
                                        of 1676: a Critical Edition* (Records of Social
                                        and Economic History, n.s. 10, 1986)

Conford, '*Organic society*'   P. Conford, 'Organic society: agriculture and
                                        radical politics in the career of Gerard Wallop,
                                        ninth earl of Portsmouth (1898–1984)',
                                        Agricultural History Review 53 (2005), 78–96

Conservation Area   BDBC, *Cliddesden Conservation Area Appraisal*
                                        (Basingstoke, 2003)

Crockford Clerical Dir.   Crockford's Clerical Directory

Dean and others, *Light Railway*   M. Dean, K. Robertson and R. Simmonds, *The
                                        Basingstoke and Alton Light Railway*
                                        (Crowcombe, 1998)

Design Statement   BDBC, *Cliddesden Village Design Statement*
                                        (Basingstoke, 2004)

Dioc. Pop. Returns   A. Dyer and D.M. Palliser (eds), *The Diocesan
                                        Population Returns for 1563 and 1603* (Records
                                        of Social and Economic History, n.s. 31, Oxford,
                                        2005)

Doing the Duty   Mark Smith (ed.), *Doing the Duty of the Parish:
                                        Surveys of the Church in Hampshire, 1810* (HRS
                                        17, 2004)

Domesday   A. Williams and G.H. Martin (eds.),
                                        Domesday Book: a Complete Translation
                                        (2002)

Dugdale, *Mon.*

W. Dugdale, *Monasticon Anglicanum*, ed. J. Caley and others. 6 vols (1817–30)

Educ. Enquiry Abstract

Education Enquiry: Abstract of the Answers and Returns (Parl. Papers 1835 (62) ii)

Educ. of Poor Digest

Digest of Parochial Returns on the Education of the Poor (Parl. Papers 1819 (224) ii)

Excerpta e Rot. Finium

Excerpta e Rotulis Finium, Hen. III, 2 vols (Rec. Com., 1835-6)

f(f)

folio(s)

Fasham and Keevill, *Brighton Hill*

P.J. Fasham and G. Keevill, *Brighton Hill South (Hatch Warren): an Iron Age Farmstead and Deserted Medieval Village* (Salisbury, 1995)

Feudal Aids

Inquisitions and Assessments relating to Feudal Aids preserved in the Public Record Office, 6 vols (HMSO, 1899–1920)

Glasscock (ed.), *Subsidy 1334*

R.E. Glasscock (ed.), *The Lay Subsidy of 1334* (British Academy Records of Social and Economic Hist. n.s. 2, 1975)

ha.

hectare(s)

HCC

Hampshire County Council

Hants HER

Hampshire Historic Environment Record, https://www.hants.gov.uk landplanningandenvironment/environment/ historicenvironment/historicenvironmentrecord

Hants Subsidy 1586

C.R. Davey (ed.), *The Hampshire Lay Subsidy Rolls, 1586* (HRS 4, 1981)

Hants Tax 1327

P. Mitchell-Fox and M. Page (eds), *The Hampshire Tax List of 1327* (HRS 20, 2014)

HRO

Hampshire Record Office

HRS

Hampshire Record Series

Hearth Tax

E. Hughes and P. White (eds), *The Hampshire Hearth Tax Assessment, 1665* (HRS 11, 1991)

Hist. Parl.

The History of Parliament: House of Commons (1964–)

Kelly's Dir. Hants.

Kelly's Directory of Hampshire and the Isle of Wight

Kussmaul, *Servants*

Ann Kussmaul, *Servants in Husbandry* (Cambridge, 1981)

Lipkin, *Institutions*

J.A. Lipkin, *Institutions in the Diocese of Winchester, 1487-1528*, HRO unpubl. register

MERL

Museum of English Rural Life, University of Reading

Nonarum Inquisitiones	*Nonarum Inquisitiones in Curia Scaccarii* (Rec. Com., 1807)
n.d.	no date
NHLE	National Heritage List for England, https://historicengland.org.uk/listing/the-list/
n.s.	new series
ODNB	*Oxford Dictionary of National Biography* (Oxford, 2004); www.oxforddnb.com
OS	Ordnance Survey
PO Dir. Hants.	*Post Office Directory of Hampshire, Wiltshire and Dorset*
PRS	Pipe Roll Society
Parl. Papers	Parliamentary Papers
Parson and Parish	W.R. Ward (ed.), *Parson and Parish in Eighteenth Century Hampshire: Replies to Bishops' Visitations* (HRS 13, 1995)
pers. comm.	personal communication
Pevsner, *North Hampshire*	M. Bullen, J. Crook, R.Hubbuck and N. Pevsner (eds), *The Buildings of England: Hampshire: Winchester and the North* (2010)
Pipe R	*Pipe Roll*
Placit. in Domo Capit. Abbrev.	*Placitorum in Domo Capitulari Westmonasteriensi Asservatorum Abbreviatio* (Rec. Com., 1811)
Poor Abstract, 1777	*Report from the Committee Appointed to Inspect and Consider the Returns made by the Overseers of the Poor ... together with Abstracts of the said Returns* (Parl. Papers 1777)
Poor Abstract, 1804	*Abstract of Answers and Returns ... Relative to Expense and Maintenance of the Poor* (Parl. Papers 1804 (175))
Poor Rate Rtns, 1822, 1835	*Select Committee on Poor Rate Returns: Reports* (Parl. Papers 1822 (556); 1835 (444))
Poor Rate Rtns, 1837, 1838	*Poor Law Commissioners: Third and Fourth Annual Reports* (Parl. Papers 1837 (546); 1838 (147))
Proc. Hants F.C.	*Proceedings of the Hampshire Field Club and Archaeological Society*
r.	rod(s)
Rec. Com.	Record Commission

Reg. Beaufort	HRO, 21M65/A1/12: register of Henry, Cardinal Beaufort
Reg. Bilson	HRO, 21M65/A1/29: register of Thomas Bilson
Reg. Courtney	HRO, 21M65/A1/15: register of Peter Courtney
Reg. Edington	S.F. Hockey (ed.), *The Register of William Edington, Bishop of Winchester 1346–1366*, 2 vols (HRS 7–8, 1986–7)
Reg. Horne	HRO, 21M65/A1/26: register of Robert Horne
Reg. Morley	HRO, 21M65/A1/33: register of George Morley
Reg. Orleton	HRO, 21M65/A1/6–7: register of Adam de Orleton I–II
Regs. Sandale and Asser	F.J. Baigent (ed.), *John de Sandale and Rigaud de Asserio AD 1316–25, Episcopal Registers: Diocese of Winchester* (HRS, 1897)
Reg. Stratford	R.M. Haines (ed.), *The Register of John de Stratford, Bishop of Winchester 1323–33*, 2 vols (SRS 42–3, 2010–11)
Reg. Waynflete	HRO, 21M65/A1/13–14: register of William Waynflete I–II
Reg. Woodlock	A.W. Goodman (ed.), *Registrum Henrici Woodlock, Diocesis Wintoniensis, A.D. 1305–1316*, 2 vols (Oxford, 1940–1).
Reg. Wykeham	T.F. Kirby (ed.), *Wykeham's Register,* 2 vols (HRS, 1896–9)
Rel. Census	J.A. Vickers, *The Religious Census of 1851* (HRS 12, 1993)
Rtn of Parishes	*Return of Civil Parishes in England and Wales under the Education Act* (Parl. Papers 1871 (201))
rot.	rotulet
Rot. Hund.	*Rotuli Hundredorum,* 2 vols (Rec. Com., 1812–18)
School Boards	*Board of Education: List of School Boards and School Attendance Committees in England and Wales* (Parl. Papers 1901 [Cd. 487])
School Inquiry	*Royal Commission to Inquire into Education in Schools in England and Wales* (Parl. Papers 1868 (3966-x) xi)
Tax. Eccl.	*Taxatio Ecclesiastica Angliae et Walliae auctoritate Papae Nicholai IV, c.1291* London, (Rec. Com., 1802)
TNA	The National Archives

unpubl.	unpublished
Valor Eccl.	*Valor Ecclesiasticus, temp. Henrici VIII*, 6 vols (Rec. Com., 1810–34)
VCH	*Victoria County History*
WCL	Winchester Cathedral Library
Wallop, *Knot of Roots*	G.V. Wallop, *A Knot of Roots: an Autobiography* (1965)
Watney, *Wallop Family*	V.J. Watney, *The Wallop Family and their Ancestry*, 4 vols (Oxford, 1928)
White's Dir.	W. White, *History, Gazetteer, and Directory of Hampshire and the Isle of Wight*

GLOSSARY

Aisle (side and hip): in some timber-framed buildings, a range running along one or both sides or ends of a space open to the roof and covered by continuations of the roof.

Churchwardens: officials responsible for the church fabric and contents, who answer to the archdeacon for the affairs of the parish.

Draught: a type of heavy patterned cloth.

Kersey: coarse narrow ribbed woollen cloth woven from long wool, originally from Kersey in Suffolk.

Overseers of the poor: officers charged with relief of those in need.

Scraw: frame upon which textile fabrics were hung to dry.

Sheer: a type of light see-through cloth.

Teg: a sheep in its second year.

Tod: approximately 28 lbs of wool.

View of frankpledge: the court held at Basingstoke twice a year for the town and parishes of the hundred.

Watchet: light blue colour, cloth or garment of this colour, originally from Watchet in Somerset.

CPSIA information can be obtained
at www.ICGtesting.com
Printed in the USA
JSHW022225211219
3115JS00002B/13

9 781912 702008